HELP!
MY BUSINESS IS HOLDING ME HOSTAGE

HELP!
MY BUSINESS IS HOLDING ME HOSTAGE

Three steps to finding your exit while discovering the new and improved you!

Copyright © 2021 LaToya R. Thurmond, PhD

Title: Help My Business Is Holding Me Hostage
Subtitle: Three steps to finding your exit while discovering the new and improved you!

ISBN: 978-1-952327-74-2

All rights reserved. No part of this book may be reproduced or transmitted in any form or by any means without written permission from the author.

T.A.L.K. Publishing
5215 North Ironwood Road, Suite 200
Glendale, WI 53217
myauthorlab.com

CONTENTS

Foreword 7
Acknowledgments 9
Introduction 11

Chapter 1   Every Problem Has A Solution 13
Chapter 2   Freedom 21
Chapter 3   Captivity 30
Chapter 4   The Voice of the Critic 38
Chapter 5   Identity 53
Chapter 6   Ticking Time Bomb 60
Chapter 7   Find Your Moment of Meaning 73
Chapter 8   Escape Plan 78
Chapter 9   Realization 85
Chapter 10   Refocus 98
Chapter 11   Relaunch 135
Chapter 12   Conclusion 152

Definition of Terms 155
References 157

FOREWORD

Dr. LaToya Thurmond has penned a timeless masterpiece. Every business owner will find themselves in the very situation that Dr. LaToya describes in her book *Help! My Business Is Holding Me Hostage*, often without direction or words to express what they are going through. Dr. LaToya put on paper exactly what they will experience but more so. Because of her own experience life has given her from years of hard work, she is able to give them the direction they need, step by step. Her guidance and wisdom will help them to clearly navigate the process and find their way out of the bondage of being held hostage by their business.

We've traveled to over twenty-eight countries of the world and over ninety cities in the United States. One thing that we've seen by experience is that many business owners do not have mentors and the training necessary to navigate difficult places in their career. Dr. LaToya gives wisdom and direction to every entrepreneur and gives great attention to detail and instruction in navigating difficult places in business. We've written over twenty books, and we've been teaching leadership all over the world. I spent thirteen years in the US Army. My wife has a bachelor's in leadership from the University of South Florida, an MBA from Southeastern University, and she's the chairman of the board of directors for one of the largest charter management organizations in the world. We've yet to read anything like what Dr. LaToya has written concerning business and entrepreneurship.

It's our opinion that Dr. LaToya's experience makes her the right person to write this book. She details that after years of stagnation, blurred vision, and burnout, she saw the need for change. This is a process that you would have to have gone through to develop this kind of knowledge. Unfortunately, you cannot get it from just watching someone else's life or even from hearing their testimony. It must be something you've lived out.

One of my favorite passages from one of my favorite books describes a mentor telling his mentee that he had traveled with him and firsthand observed the process that he himself had endured. Paul tells Timothy in that he had fully known his process. He goes on to say, "But you have observed my doctrine manner of life, purpose, faith, tolerance, love, patience, persecutions and afflictions which came unto me at Antioch, Iconium, and Lystra what persecutions I endured" (2 Timothy 3:10 MEV). He uses the word "fully known" in the original text of the King James Bible, which when translated is the Greek word *parakoluntheo*, which means to follow closely a mental trail clearly set forth by one who has clearly traveled the terrain, investigated every detail, and left no stone unturned. Dr. LaToya is a wise mentor teaching every entrepreneur and business owner who will submit themselves to her masterful tutelage. She's learned and has earned the T-shirt she's asking them to buy. She has mastered her craft and wants to help others not make the mistakes that she herself has made.

Everyone who reads this book will be given the tools necessary to navigate and succeed in their business endeavors. At the end of the day that's what it's all about, succeeding in what you feel is your purpose and destiny. Dr. LaToya gives you the tools to navigate and not fall into the pitfalls that every leader will eventually be faced with.

—*LaJun and Valora Cole*
President & CEO of Cole & Company Global;
Founders and Senior Leaders of LaJun & Valora Cole Ministries and Contagious Church; Authors of *Sudden Breakthrough* and *Divine Dispatch: Discover, Develop, and Deploy Your Given Assignment*

ACKNOWLEDGMENTS

This book is dedicated to my husband, Shaun, and daughters, Arion and Shia. You all have remained present with me during my physical and mental hiatus. I am grateful for your unconditional love and patience. Shaun, thank you for always rescuing me from the zone and showing me what matters most in life. I definitely could not have done this without your selfless love, support, and honesty.

Lord only knows that I felt like I was losing my mind at some points, as I often suffered in silence. I am a witness to God's unfailing love and provision throughout my wilderness experience. I will be forever grateful for the divine alignments and amazing staff, mentors, and confidants that God sent throughout my sixteen-year entrepreneurial journey.

I would like to thank all the entrepreneurs who have contributed their reflections and insight to the Freedom chapter. Your knowledge and experiences are invaluable. I thank you for your contribution and support and for believing in this project. I would like to thank Apostle LaJun and Prophetess Valora Cole of LaJun and Valora Cole Ministries for all their genuine love, support, and commitment to my continuous growth and development. You have truly helped me to see my calling and gifting to marketplace ministry in a new light. Thank you for pushing me to pursue and exceed my full potential, destiny, purpose, and rightful place. I am grateful to have been placed in the care of such amazing and loving leaders.

Thank you to my editor, Libby Gontarz. I cannot thank you enough for your patience, encouragement, honest feedback, and great attention to detail. Your patience, peace, love, and kindness were felt each session. You revived my excitement for the project after what seemed like a long journey full of twist and turns.

Finally, thank you, Jolanda Rogers and the T.A.L.K. Publishing team for pushing this project to the finish line. You and your team moved in rapid speed in helping me to recover lost time. Thank you for helping me to achieve my dream of completing this project and your commitment to publishing in a spirit of excellence.

INTRODUCTION

Balancing business and motherhood has been a constant struggle.

As a mom, wife, entrepreneur, and full-time career student, I found that twenty-four hours in a day was never enough. I began working in my father's family-owned business as an administrative assistant which led to me working as an accounts payable clerk and human resource coordinator to eventually operations manager where I oversaw the performance of five locations with approximately 100 employees.

I founded a new business with a partner who focused more on her family life while I focused more on the business. That imbalance in business philosophies led to a dissolving of the partnership. It also caused a personal rift between us, which was especially unfortunate because my business partner was my sister. My dedication to my business also negatively affected my physical health and home life. A business crisis caused me to reevaluate and relaunch a new and improved me.

I would like to share what I have learned with you to help you achieve true business and life success.

What, besides my own failure and lessons learned, qualifies me to do so?

Experience is sometimes the best teacher. My entrepreneurial experience and education have allowed me to coach entrepreneurs in the area of business start-up and navigating challenges. I earned a Bachelor's in Business Administration from the University of Wisconsin—Parkside, a Master's in Adult Education from the University of Wisconsin—Platteville, and a PhD from Capella

University in Industrial-Organizational Psychology. My doctoral work addresses the need to identify coping strategies that help entrepreneurs move beyond the point of failure to the point of learning and applying the lessons learned through the 3R Redemptive Model: Realization, Refocus, and Rebirth.

Help! My Business is Holding Me Hostage is for any business owner who feels they have grown stagnant and feels trapped. This book takes you on a personal journey through work obsession, business crises, and how to break free. At the end of each section, you will be encouraged to complete exercises that will challenge you to evaluate your personal wellbeing and the business.

The first half of the book identifies challenges and barriers that have a negative impact on your overall well-being, which in turn has a direct effect on your business. The second half of the book will lead you in identifying solutions that will move you beyond your position of stagnation to your exit. I will be referencing my personal business experiences throughout this book. *Help! My Business Is Holding Me Hostage* will challenge you to think inwardly to evaluate your mental, emotional, and physical state to determine if you are in a state of danger and, if not, how to avoid getting there. Finally, it helps you identify and evaluate the lessons you have learned so you can apply them to reviving a struggling business, starting a new business, or discovering a new career path.

What you are about to read is my entrepreneurial experience and path to transformation. After years of stagnation, blurred vision, and burnout, I eventually saw the need for change. I desperately needed an exit strategy from the business that bound me. I needed freedom. You may be in a similar situation. This book will guide you in developing an exit strategy that will lead to your own greater personal freedom, whether you adjust your business's demands on your life or leave entrepreneurship behind.

CHAPTER 1

EVERY PROBLEM HAS A SOLUTION

If you are unwilling to change, your business will never be capable of giving you what you want.

—Michael E. Gerber

Raising two beautiful girls has been the greatest part of my life's journey; however, balancing business and motherhood has been a constant struggle. Long days, unexpected crises, and business challenges were consistently at war with concerts, dance recitals, and soccer games. My husband watched me pour most of my time and energy into the business and wanted no part of what he would call chaos. While I wanted a successful business, he wanted a normal family life for our daughters. Normalcy included both of us working stable jobs that would provide financially and not interfere with family time. Unfortunately, the first ten years of business required hard work, sacrifice, and constant interruptions that made it hard for me to remain present. Learning to balance a family and business also included journeying through two academic programs over a span of fourteen years. Twenty-four hours in a day was simply never enough.

I began working in my father's family-owned business, One Step Ahead, Inc., in 1998. I worked as an administrative assistant, accounts payable clerk, human resource coordinator, and finally as operations manager. Having the responsibility of overseeing five childcare facilities that employed approximately one hundred employees throughout southeast Wisconsin prepared me for my future entrepreneurial journey. This experience would later provide me with the necessary skills, knowledge, and resilience to survive in business during an economic crisis.

In 2005, my sister Preneice Love and I co-founded LaPre Enterprise, birthed out of One Step Ahead. My father had chosen to retire from the business and left two centers in our care. As sisters, we continued to build on the solid foundation of my father's vision of providing quality childcare, employment opportunities, and family support services throughout southeast Wisconsin.

Shortly after the inception of LaPre Enterprise, we noticed a shift in regulations at the state level that would require a change in how we managed the business. As we took note of the change in the industry, we quickly adjusted and developed new strategies and innovative ideas. Those adjustments included working longer days and nights in the operation, building stronger relationships with our staff, managing business challenges, researching, and learning more about the unexpected shift in the childcare industry.

Although the business was progressing, my sister and I began to experience a strain in our relationship. We shared quite different viewpoints as to the level of commitment and what was necessary to achieve business success. I was content with opening and closing, running nonstop, not having a set schedule of when I would be able to go home, handling complaints, listening to employee concerns, and managing administrative duties.

Preneice said she noticed a change in me two years after starting the business when I found it necessary to take phone calls from staff about an error on a payroll check—just hours after giving birth to Shia. Weeks later when I went to see my ob-gyn to have my staples removed, I left the hospital and met with a member of the management team off site to discuss some employee concerns. A month after delivery, I showed up at the title company anxious to sign loan documents for the purchase of our new building. Taking care of my health had taken a back seat to managing the operation.

Preneice stood strong on her commitment to spending quality time with family. She valued those precious moments and was in no way willing to sacrifice for a business.

At that time, I just did not understand her viewpoint. We both had little ones, and the nature of our business made it easy to include our children in everything. Whether it be opening the center because of a call-in or closing the center because of being short-staffed, we had the luxury to bring our kids along. Neither of us was willing to back down on what we felt, unwilling to waver in our personal beliefs. Our sisterhood was challenged. Our staff could sense the strain in our relationship; they were in the middle of two sisters at war. Shouting matches, hurt feelings, and bitterness led to days and weeks of not speaking to one another.

Ultimately, Preneice surrendered her ownership rights in 2008. As she moved on to do what was best for her and her family, I moved on burdened but determined to bear a much larger weight of responsibility.

The year 2009 was a great year for LaPre Enterprise. Networking led to community partnerships and the start of a teen mom mentorship program. Having been a teen mom, I understood the challenges and barriers that teenage mothers faced. The mentor program grew within the walls of LaPre Enterprise and led to the creation of A&S Unlimited Solutions, a nonprofit organization that provides resources and support services to at-risk youth, families, and providers. As I expanded my business, I was also receiving recognition at the state and national level. That year I was awarded the 2009 Small

Business Young Entrepreneur of the Year Award for the Midwest and Southeast Regions of Wisconsin.

In 2010, the downward turn of the economy had a direct impact on LaPre Enterprise. The decline in revenue and sales required a significant reduction in labor hours, which pushed me right back into the day-to-day operation. Once I noticed the significant reduction in revenue, I weaned myself off payroll. Deep cuts, layoffs, and eliminations of support staff were not enough to keep our accounts from running in the negative. Revenue was low, but the mortgage, rent, utilities, insurance, payroll, taxes, and other operational expenses were not going anywhere. I made sure our employees were paid biweekly but delayed paying payroll taxes, which continued to add up every other week.

When the business accounts were depleted, I financed the business using my personal checking and savings. However, that did not last long as everything was emptied out within two months. Depleted business and personal accounts put me in a battle with fear. At home, I was physically present, but my mind was being held captive, in constant search of solutions.

As I pridefully continued to press forward, I was no longer enjoying the entrepreneurial journey, and I felt like I was in over my head. Although I was burned-out with a faded vision, I was still obsessed with achieving business success. Unaware of my stagnation, I somehow convinced myself that all I needed to do was show up, make sure the day went smoothly, increase enrollment, and keep driving the expenses down.

In search of opportunity during times of struggle, I created LMT Consulting, LLC, in 2011. This challenged me to step outside of my comfort zone to use my unique skill set and education to overcome my personal financial struggles.

Ultimately, it took a business crisis to help me see the need for change. In 2015, one of our locations experienced a fire and a flood over the weekend. While this crippled my business, I experienced an awakening that led me on the path to rediscovering a new and improved me.

Problem Statement

For many business owners, the key benefit of entrepreneurship is freedom: freedom from working on someone else's schedule, freedom from a boss, and freedom to let their creativity flourish. At some point, however, you may have felt that your business was doing the exact opposite: holding you hostage rather than granting you freedom.

Do you feel like your desire to discontinue your business to gain freedom contradicts the key benefit of entrepreneurship? Are you experiencing fear of financial instability? Has the idea of starting a new career path left you in total distress? Does the thought of reporting to a boss give you nightmares?

Coming to the point of choosing whether to hold on or let go of your company can include a constant and overwhelming flow of emotions. Ultimately, your decision should be predicated upon the goals you have set for your business and your plans for departure. If you have overlooked the exit planning of your business, you may have found yourself in a place of stagnation.

If you are reading this book because you are looking to start a business, kudos to you for taking time to explore the importance of planning ahead for your grand exit. On the other hand, you may have already experienced the rewarding feeling of creating and managing a business. Perhaps you developed a unique solution to a problem, with great intentions of serving your community, country, or maybe even the world. You likely put in overtime working hard to build a brand that defines your business and sets it apart from competitors. Hopefully, after all your hard work, you achieved growth, maximum profits, and expansion. Now, however, you may feel that the achievement of accomplishing all your goals has left you with nothing else to give. Yet you cannot seem to let go and take your final bow.

According to Lee, Jasper, and Goebel (2003), business owners' departure and progression may include transferring the businesses' possessions to the next generation, selling the company, or closing the operation.[1] You may have inherited the family business and planned to take the organization to the next level. You were trusted to maintain the business and perhaps wrestled with relinquishing control, fearing family disappointment. The responsibility of accepting the organization from your predecessor may feel like a heavy burden. Still, you have held on to the family business. Holding on to something that you no longer desire, however, can be mentally, physically, and emotionally draining.

Perhaps the operation is not performing as you have anticipated, and you are not sure what to do. You are being drained financially and psychologically while your "inner critic" has convinced you that letting go of the business would mean you have failed. Our inner critics are geniuses at formulating negative opinions, finding fault, and judging decisions to make us fall prey to self-doubt.

Your inner critic is not discriminatory. It will harass you with thoughts of fear and failure if you are thinking about starting a business. On the other hand, it will downplay your accomplishments and have you on a constant pursuit of success.

I am very familiar with the heckling of the inner critic—the voice that troubles you throughout the day as you imagine an alternate life without your business. At the same time, imagining life without your business results in a crippling fear of failure. It's a never-ending cycle of what-ifs. Imprisoned by impending consequences and fear of failure, you forfeit your freedom and become a hostage to your work.

---

[1] Yoon Lee, Cynthia R. Jasper, and Karen Goebel, *A Profile of Succession Planning Among Family Business Owners* (*Journal of Financial Counseling and Planning*, Vol. 14, No. 2, 2003). Available at SSRN: https://ssrn.com/abstract=2265569

Learning to contend with negative emotions aroused by your inner critic requires that you first realize its existence. Once you realize that you are dealing with negative emotions, you can then acknowledge your struggle and make a commitment to not allow those emotions to control you. This will involve a great level of self-awareness, taking time to unplug from the hustle and bustle, emptying out your thoughts through journaling, and giving yourself some grace. Mike Murdock (2002) says, "When you change your focus, you will change your feelings." Focusing on what could be instead of what is gives you the motivation to push forward with creating an exit strategy using short- and long-term goals.

Solution Overview

"Identify your problems but give your power and energy to solutions," Tony Robbins has said.

What you are about to read is my entrepreneurial experience and path to transformation. After years of stagnation, blurred vision, and burnout, I eventually saw the need for change. LaPre Enterprise was underperforming, and I was stuck in the monotony. The constant struggle became normal, and I could not imagine life without it.

Realization of the need for change came through a crisis. A fire and flood completely ravaged one of the two locations. Unsure if the organization would survive, I worked hard to research, strategize, and resolve issues—anything to save my business. At the same time, I was challenged by negative emotions and ongoing business crises. While I struggled to save the company, my husband and daughters suffered silently. Canceled dinner plans, late arrivals to concerts, and constantly interrupted focus weighed heavily on my family.

Throughout this book, I will demonstrate how all the negativity led me to a place of realization and refocus, and how I was eventually able to relaunch myself, both personally and professionally, to live a balanced life beyond business challenges.

My hope is that this book will help fellow entrepreneurs to avoid the physical and mental turmoil that I experienced, or else to provide the tools to find an escape if you are already held captive to your business.

As you will soon see, my life was like an emotional rollercoaster full of twists, turns, and neglect. Based on my work with other entrepreneurs, my personal accounts are relatable and will help you recognize the need for change. This book includes engaging exercises that consist of tools and tips that will move you from a place of self-imprisonment to discovering life beyond the hustle. Through a process of realization, refocus, and relaunch, you will discover how to exit your business when you're ready while also rediscovering *you*!

CHAPTER 2

FREEDOM

Everything that is really great and inspiring is created by the individual who can labor in freedom.
—Albert Einstein

Wikipedia defines freedom as having the ability to act or change without constraint. There can be a sense of restriction when someone feels that they are tethered to a nine-to-five job. The exploratory journey of entrepreneurship can be predicated on the desire for freedom.

The liberty of working for yourself comes with many advantages that can help you achieve personal and professional goals. Your decision to start a business may have been so you could build a legacy to pass on to future generations. Perhaps you were intrigued by the idea of setting your own schedule solely to spend more time with family. On the other hand, you may have simply identified a problem and wanted to provide the solution.

Among the many reasons people want to leave traditional day jobs, the work environment is often a top offender. It's easy to be silenced among crowds of coworkers and superiors. Perhaps you even had a clear vision of how you would initiate change by transforming the workplace culture to improve communications; however, your ideas continued to be ignored. Perhaps you desire an ability to think freely without being controlled by a micromanaging, insecure boss. You may have found the workplace to be mentally exhausting as you tried to embrace workplace culture and its method of thinking.

The freedom you have as an entrepreneur allows you to create your ideal environment for employees, customers, and everyone else involved. Instead of spending your energy on mental games, as an entrepreneur you can use your creative mindset to help others resolve problems.

Whatever the reasoning for starting or taking over your own business, chances are the desire to be free was a top priority.

In the following section, five entrepreneurs share their thoughts on the idea of freedom when self-employed. In question-and-answer format, you will learn directly from these entrepreneurs with varying levels of experience in several different industries.

Each entrepreneur is introduced by name, industry, and time spent self-employed.

LaShon Stevens, Real Estate Agent, 1 Year of Entrepreneurial Experience

Q: How do you define freedom as an entrepreneur?
A: Freedom as an entrepreneur is realizing each day that I am my own boss and that no other person is the steward of my career endeavors. I am responsible for managing my business, my schedule, working hours, production rate, financial affairs, etc. I am ensuring the legacy and well-being of my family, and I shall reap the benefits of my own hearty work ethic.
Q: What freedoms have you gained as an entrepreneur?
A: I create my own work schedule, which frees me from the nine-to-five grind. As an entrepreneur, I am constantly improving my skills to ensure that my business succeeds. I'm free to work

with whomever I please, which has placed me in the paths of many like-minded individuals. I'd be remiss if I didn't mention the freedom I've gained to create wealth for myself. In my first ninety days as an entrepreneur, I grossed what I made in the previous six months as an employee.

Q: What freedoms have you lost as an entrepreneur, if any?

A: I'm not quite sure if I've lost any freedoms, or maybe I'm just unable to articulate them at this moment. Business is going well for me! However, being the chief decision-maker day in and day out isn't all good; it has been stressful.

Bitha Bell, Beauty Salon & Realty Owner, 10 Years of Entrepreneurial Experience

Q: How do you define freedom as an entrepreneur?

A: In my field, the most valuable freedom that I have is expression. I get to express myself in and outside of the salon through words, creativity, and fashion without being worried about if I am breaking a code. Where there are pros, there are cons.

Q: What freedoms have you gained as an entrepreneur?

A: As an entrepreneur I have been able to attend school events, conferences, doctor appointments, and sporting events without having to put in for time off. I have also been able to enjoy networking with other entrepreneurs, oftentimes bouncing ideas off one another.

Q: What freedoms have you lost as an entrepreneur, if any?

A: When I became a business owner, everything I did or said was reflected directly onto my business. People tend to have a hard time separating the two. It's not bad enough for me to want to stop, though. I have just had to learn how to finesse my way through so that I am able to be me as a person and a business without being judged terribly for it.

Lisa Parham, Newspaper Publisher, 15 Years of Entrepreneurial Experience

Q: How do you define freedom as an entrepreneur?

A: I find it rewarding and exciting and at times challenging. I'm excited for what's happening in my life in the limelight and behind the scenes. I love what I do.

Q: What freedoms have you gained as an entrepreneur?

A: The freedom that I gained was being able to do what I enjoy doing. I went into business with the expectation of being my own boss, setting my own hours, and supposedly working on my own terms. However, let's be honest about small business ownership. It's really difficult at times to succeed; I know because I've been there a time or two, and it has been painful as well as frustrating. The reality of being a business owner turned out to be much different than I expected. I thought I would never have to punch another clock, but being my own boss I've come to realize punching the clock never stops. I've had to learn how to create a successful business while living life on my terms. I have also gained freedom in being able to influence and inspire the lives of individuals I come into contact with on a daily basis such as families, employees, and customers.

Q: What freedoms have you lost as an entrepreneur, if any?

A: To me, freedom lost is freedom gained. Someone might say, *If starting and running a business is so difficult, then why do it?* Success has a profound impact on your inner strength. There are many lonely moments when you are trying to start a business or get your vision off the ground. Another difficult component is the incredible amount of mental energy one has to dedicate.

Mary Xiong, Strategic Business Coach, 13 Years of Entrepreneurial Experience

Q: How do you define freedom as an entrepreneur?

A: As a small business owner and entrepreneur, I define freedom as the ability to have choices to grow, to create a work culture that prioritizes one's values and encourages one's ability to meet one's ever-growing potential.

Q: What freedoms have you gained as an entrepreneur?

A: In my experience, I believe I have gained freedom in how I use my time, process my goals and dreams, challenge myself to continuously push my personal and professional boundaries, to believe in what I value and be authentic to that with no boundaries, and to encourage healthy and positive change.

Q: What freedoms have you lost as an entrepreneur, if any?

A: I would not consider what I lost as a freedom, but I have lost the comfort of working for a paycheck, waiting for others to lead me and the vision, blaming others for my circumstances, and complaining about others' abilities and carelessness.

Brent Oglesby, Real Estate Developer, 17 Years of Entrepreneurial Experience

Q: How do you define freedom as an entrepreneur?

A: My definition of freedom has changed with time. In my late teens and early twenties, I believed freedom for me exclusively meant financial success. One of my earliest goals was to be a millionaire before I turned thirty. With time and experience I appreciated that freedom and assets are so much more than cash. Currently a significant part of freedom for me is control of my time, ability to selectively work on projects which resonate with me and bringing my entire self to my work. I realized making and earning money, even significant money, is the easy part of all this. Relationships, time, health, improving your communities, and many other things are exceptionally more important now.

Q: What freedoms have you gained as an entrepreneur?

A: I came back to this question last because a part of me truly questioned had I gained anything as an entrepreneur. That or I just needed time to step back and think about the last twenty years and think about what I gained from a more unbiased perspective. Control of my time is probably the greatest part of or gain from being an entrepreneur. For example, if I needed a break in the middle of the day, I could play tennis for two hours, clear my mind, and come back even more productive. Granted, I did not do this as much as I would have liked. Additionally, I have worked with some truly brilliant, inspiring, and motivated entrepreneurs. Those teams and individuals will always have a special place in my heart. Entrepreneurship has also allowed me to be exposed to and learn so much. As a lifelong learner these lessons quite possibly are invaluable.

A final benefit for me has been the ability to be relatively unrestricted in my physical travels. Working from Sydney, Australia, for a month because I needed a break, spending weeks in Los Angeles, time in Jamaica, trips to Toronto, sunshine in Miami, attending my son's out-of-state basketball tournaments, and so many months in the red clay of Georgia. Those times provided me some of my most creative and productive moments. The ability to think and create at my own pace is really, or has been, the most luxurious part of being an entrepreneur.

Q: What freedoms have you lost as an entrepreneur, if any?

A: Some freedoms I have lost as an entrepreneur include investing significantly more time into creating and growing ventures than deeply enjoying my life. Additionally, I have left numerous personal and professional relationships due to feeling many people couldn't relate to my drive. When I think back to the years and years of eighty to 120-hour workweeks, I lost a lot of time appreciating life. Also, if I'm being honest with myself, I've lost probably two other things. One I could have possibly easily replicated, that being the ability to work with powerful teams. Two, and potentially in my situation the most frustrating, is I've lost a significant amount of capital as well as potential capital from taking on projects I should have passed on or passed off. I often question, or have questioned, if it would have been easier to just find a job, stack up a few million, and be retired by forty.

Final Reflection

Freedom provides you with the right to choose. Whether it be how you choose to spend your day or how you create your future, the choice is yours. However, your ability to choose does not guarantee a stress-free life. What looks like freedom to you may not represent freedom to someone else. Your pursuit of freedom may even cost you your freedom. Managing a business can knock you down, but the freedom to choose is what gets you back up. Freedom is believing that your identity is not defined by the nine-to-five. Faith gives you the freedom to create your own path while journeying into the unknown. Marching to the beat of your own drum allows you to walk in your freedom by embracing the authentic you.

Are You Being Held Hostage?

Time has the potential to be a gift and a curse. There is freedom in having time to spend with family and friends. On the other hand, time must be sacrificed in exchange for hard work and success. Ultimately, time management and finding balance is the key to freedom.

Upon establishing why you were going into business, you most likely spent some time thinking about what you wanted to achieve.

Whether a particular amount of revenue, accumulation of assets, or just a wealth generator for your children, you had something in mind. Your ideas morphed into goals, which most likely transferred into a solid business plan. This included particulars pertaining to timelines and the resources and tools it would take to accomplish your goals. Eventually, you discovered that the road to achieving your business goals can be challenging. There is no guarantee you will achieve them. Ultimately, you came to an intersection where you have to make decisions about what path you will follow next.

Stop and think: What is the catalyst to your freedom?

Through a process of realization and refocus you will be moving forward in no time! This book has been designed with you in mind and will serve as your guide to rediscovering the new and improved you.

Guidelines:

1. Read and work through the exercises at your own pace.

2. Carefully think about each question and how it relates to your current situation.

3. Be honest with yourself.

4. Commit to a new mindset that will push you forward.

5. Make a mental note of the lessons that you have learned throughout your journey.

At this time, stop and reflect on the hurdles in your life and career that block your path to freedom.

Freedom

Provide examples of how your business provides you the freedom to think.

If it does not provide you with freedom to think, please share why it does not.

Using only one or two words, list the five ways you desired to gain freedom in starting your business (Example: flexible hours)

1._____

2._____

3._____

4._____

5._____

CHAPTER 3

CAPTIVITY

What we think of as our refuge and sanctuary could easily become the place of our captivity.

—Mladen Dordevic

If my business could talk, I think it would have said, "Do exactly what I tell you and you will survive." Merriam-Webster defines *captor* as "one that has captured a person or thing."[2] In time, I found myself captured and in a constant mode of survival.

Although entrepreneurship is highly sought after, take into consideration the possibilities of it having a darker side (Miller, 2015). It often involves working in unstable work environments that include completing a wide range of tasks that entrepreneurs are not always well trained to do (Baron, 2008). You eventually discover that in time you are working more hours than you can count and maybe will not be compensated for. If you are not careful and fail to remain in control, you will quickly find yourself bound to your organization.

---

[2] Merriam-Webster.com Dictionary, Merriam-Webster, https://www.merriam-webster.com/dictiponary/captor. Accessed 23 Oct. 2021

CAPTIVITY

You may still wonder how entrepreneurs find themselves in a hostage situation. While commitment is key to your entrepreneurial success, be cautious not to cross the line into total obsession. When you move from commitment to obsession, you are most likely surrendering your identity to the business. Once your business establishes permanent occupancy in your mind, you are in captivity.

This self-imprisonment will consume you mentally, physically, and emotionally. The business will demand your undivided attention until it reaches its goal of success. Success can be identified as accomplishing a goal or purpose. Unless you have started this journey knowing what you consider success, the business may impress upon you a spirit of dissatisfaction. If you have failed to identify future goals and an exit strategy for your business, it will place you on a never-ending hamster wheel. You will be compelled to meet its demands and will enter a place of complacency.

In some bizarre way, being in a place of captivity can feel satisfying. You give your business your undivided attention even if it interferes with your personal time. There is no room for negotiation because the business must achieve the ultimate payout of success. Remember, commitment is key to success, but you may be in danger when you find yourself in a place of obsession and your business has become your idol. Your loyalty may prevent you from breaking free.

Being held captive to your business can be considered a form of Stockholm syndrome. In 1973, four hostages were held captive during a bank robbery in Stockholm, Sweden. Many most likely found it surprising that when the victims went to court, they defended and refused to testify against their captors. Stockholm syndrome describes when a victim develops feelings of trust or affection towards their subduer; in the same way, an entrepreneur can develop a loyalty to the business that is holding them hostage. Take heed of your feelings of trust and affection towards your business and all its many promises.

You May Be in Imminent Danger and Not Realize It!

In some hostage situations, the captor ended the lives of captives. In the same way, if you lose control, your business has the potential to destroy your health, family relationships, friendships, peace, and mental wellness. Researchers report that almost 37 percent of small and medium business owners report high psychological distress (Spivack and Mckelvie, 2018).

Physical Health

When you are in constant motion, it is easy to ignore your well-being by forgoing your annual checkups. Scheduled appointments, healthy eating, and exercise are overlooked due to meeting pressing business tasks and responsibilities. Research finds that as business owners put in extra work to accomplish goals, they disregard their basic health needs such as diet and exercise (Goldsby, Kuratko, & Bishop, 2005). As you continue to neglect your health, the captor will convince you that all is well and there are greater issues beyond your physical well-being. Internally you will hear something that sounds like *You have so much to accomplish and you don't feel sick. Let's just put off that appointment for another time.* What you most likely are ignoring is the direct impact that stress has on your body. According to Cardon & Patel (2015), stress can cause health challenges including high blood pressure, weight gain, and unstable coping through smoking or drinking.

Mental Wellness

If you have not yet experienced stress running your business, you will eventually. Stress happens at the point when a person faces a situation that directly affects their well-being and that burdens their personal resources (Folkman & Lazarus, 1985). I found myself stressed when I was unable to meet the payroll and had to pay employees from my personal funds. My stress level increased as my personal resources diminished right before my eyes.

Whereas organizations work in teams to resolve challenges, entrepreneurs, especially in the early stages of running the business, are often left to resolve issues independently. Managing multiple roles and responsibilities can be overwhelming and can have a direct impact on one's mental wellness. Research suggests that though entrepreneurs understand the substantial hours and energy that a business requires, they may not recognize the added stress, strain, and physical consequences it brings (Cardon & Patel, 2015).

Relationships

When I began running my business, I hardly had time for extended family and surely not anyone beyond. Everything revolved around the business, and the staff became my new family since I spent much of my time at the location outside of the weekends. The children of staff saw me as an extension of their family too as I became affectionately recognized as Ti-Ti Toya to a few.

Family relationships were fractured as I had no time for extended family events or functions, and perhaps I really did not want to make time because it would take me away from all the work that needed to be done. My responsibilities and worries distanced me from anything and anyone beyond our location and my absence was often misunderstood. Conversations with my parents included nothing more than what was happening at the business. My father became a sounding board for my financial troubles, but our brief conversations or a quick shift in the conversation was an indicator that he, too, grew tired of hearing about the struggles.

I would occasionally try to connect with friends, but it just always felt so awkward. While they were excited about building families and new career paths, much of my conversation focused on business challenges. It got to the point where my childhood best friend became my sounding board. Our conversations revolved around my staff, business success and pitfalls, and everything in between.

Without realizing it, my friends became my business coaches and counselors. I had become selfish, needing to dominate the conversations. While good friends will want to support you by listening to rants about the job or panic sessions about big decisions, they also want you to be present during social gatherings and take the time to enjoy yourself and care for others.

Are You Being Held Hostage?

Your business can hold you hostage and can disguise itself as wanting to see you and the business succeed. Total dedication to the business can evolve into obsession. When you put your total trust in the business for your personal and professional success, your mind and body become imprisoned, and you sacrifice valuable time spent with family and friends—and unfortunately your mental and physical wellbeing.

Before you can make responsible decisions, such as creating an exit plan, you must first recognize whether your business is holding you hostage. Once you admit that you are being held captive, you can then address the issues and challenges that are contributing to your unhealthy mental and physical state. Not only will you improve your overall lifestyle, but you will also be one step closer to personal and professional freedom.

We have spent this chapter defining a hostage situation and learning to admit if you are in captivity. As we progress through this book, we will work on refocusing and repositioning yourself for a relaunch of a new and improved you.

Captivity

Captivity can be defined as being imprisoned or confined.

It is difficult to see your way out when you are in too deep. This section allows you to have moments of self-reflection. You must think carefully about each question and answer them truthfully.

Can you relate to feeling imprisoned or confined to your business? If so, in what way?

THINGS TO CONSIDER:

What does business success look like to you?

What does your personal success look like to you?

Let's be honest! Can you think of any ways you may have lost sight of what it means to be a success personally?

Think about what you have sacrificed throughout your entrepreneurial journey. Check off the areas you have sacrificed:

- ☐ Mental well-being
- ☐ Physical health
- ☐ Family
- ☐ Friends
- ☐ Opportunity

- ☐ Other:
- ☐ Other:
- ☐ Other:
- ☐ Other:
- ☐ Other:

CAPTIVITY

Review the list above and write the areas in which you have sacrificed the most. How are they being impacted?

1. What ways has your _____ *(example: mental well-being)* been impacted?

2. What ways has your _____ *(example: physical well-being)* been impacted?

3. What ways has your _____ *(example: friendships)* been impacted?

4. What ways has your _____ *(example: opportunities)* been impacted?

CHAPTER 4

THE VOICE OF THE CRITIC

Your harshest critic is always going to be yourself. Don't ignore that critic but don't give it more attention than it deserves.
—Michael Ian Black

If my business could talk, it would have said, *Look at all that garbage piled up to the top and running over. LaToya, how could you allow this to happen? What will the people driving by think? I guess they will find out that your business is struggling financially and that you are unable to pay the bills.*

I was always at war with the voice of my inner critic. It was the master at magnifying business challenges and convincing me that I was not doing enough. I must admit it won often as the voice grew louder and guilt-tripped me into believing that I could not stop until everything was perfect. To make matters worse, I was so concerned about the opinions of others that I was swimming in the dumpster just to prove to people I had it all together. That's not a metaphor—let me explain.

I had been told that if you want to know whether a business is struggling, take one look at its dumpster. Funny, right! You may be thinking, *Who has time to pay attention to these types of things?* If you are anything like I was, you take others' opinions seriously—even if they have nothing better to do than spy on your garbage dumpster.

Well, we were at a point in business where cash did not flow, and things were tight. Several accounts needed immediate attention, and we could not make good on them all. The business was heavily regulated, and some bills could not be avoided. To elude disconnects on bills that could potentially cost us our license, we chose to wait on our dumpster payment. We had been struggling for some time, and our services were suspended and required immediate payment. Staff who worked hard to push as much as they could in the dumpster would stare out the window bewildered as to why the garbage trucks were no longer removing the trash.

I always found a way to pay the restoral fee after the suspension; however, it was sometimes days before we were added back on the schedule. The looks of the dumpster always made me replay this one question: *What are people going to think when they see that garbage overflowing?* My pride would not allow me to keep an unsightly dumpster, and there seemed to be only one solution: dumpster diving.

At dusk I ran dumpster plays in my mind. I calculated how much time I needed to load up my car with trash and bring it to the city dump. Mr. Scales was an observant maintenance man on staff, and I did not want him to notice me. Although he complained about the overflow of trash, he would have chastised me for stuffing filth in my car if he would have caught me in the act. I definitely did not want this to get back to Shaun either. At the appropriate time, I pulled up to the dumpster like a thief on a dark night. As I jumped out, I took a deep breath and exhaled. If my business could talk, it would have said, *LaToya, are you really going to do what I think you're going to do? What would people think about you tossing trash into your car?*

Blocking out the voice of my inner critic, I quickly grabbed the bags and shoved them into my trunk. My method was grab, run to the car, and push. I stuffed as much as I could into the trunk and then worked my way to the back seat. It was absolutely disgusting, but I felt it had to be done for the sake of my business's reputation.

How often do you go about life engaging in activities and participating in things you do not want to do just to keep people from talking? After I made a mess of myself, I learned that folks would have an opinion whether the garbage was running over or if they would have caught me stuffing bags of trash into a luxury vehicle. People would have talked if the dumpster was empty, assuming business was slow or that we were struggling to keep employees because there was no trash in the dumpster. After my fourth round of late-night dumpster diving, I sat in my car and thought, *What in the world am I doing?*

In my moment of reflection, I asked myself the question, *Why are you doing this?* I took time to think about the extreme measure I had taken and the time I had wasted doing it. I followed up with the following questions: *Are you sincerely concerned about making more room in the dumpster? If you were concerned about the trash bags on the ground having a negative impact on the neighborhood, why didn't you ask the maintenance man for help?* As I took time to reflect on each of those questions, my answers all involved caring too much about the opinions of others. Waiting and ready for my inner critic to show up, I blurted, "Who cares? Everyone has problems and should be too concerned about their own trash and filth to be worried about mine."

Who Is the Real Critic?

My inner critic was becoming the dominant voice of my thoughts. Fear of the unknown took me to some dark places, and I saw myself at my worst. I was constantly second-guessing every decision: *If I shut down one location, could the organization survive? How would I pay my employees what was due to them if I shut down? How would I keep up with the accumulating bills? What would members of the community think?*

What would my future look like? Does choosing to leave my business mean I am a failure?

When you feel inadequate or insecure about your skills, knowledge, and abilities, you fail to imagine what could be instead of what you are experiencing and feeling in the moment. Instead, you can find yourself imagining all the negativity without realizing that you are being critical of yourself. It's easy to assume that what we feel about ourselves is what others think. People do have opinions, and sometimes they help push us forward. Critics do exist, but do not overlook your inner critic in disguise.

Pushing Past the Voice of the Inner Critic

Pushing past the voice of your inner critic will require some work. You will have to gain control by first learning the voice of your inner critic and acknowledging it for what it is. Although the voice may be loud, regain your focus and determine if something that appears like a negative can be used to improve or change the situation. Whether the critique comes from within or externally, do not reject good advice, especially from those experienced in your field who want you to succeed. Acknowledge the areas that need to be adjusted and improved and then push past the rest. Create a plan and set your plan in motion. When your inner critic shows up, stand your ground and remind yourself of your awesome plan and the steps you have taken to improve your situation. Acknowledge the difference and the changes that have been made and how much you are looking forward to seeing the end results.

Fear of the Unknown

If I shut down one location, would the business survive?

I had been dealing with the difficult decision of closing a struggling location for four months when I received great advice from other business owners who participated in my research study, "The Entrepreneurial Experience of Business Loss," to fulfill my dissertation requirements at Capella University. One participant expressed how important it was to remain present.

I needed that advice, because I just wanted to run away from it all. With fear running rampant through my mind, I would often shut down and ignore the tasks that needed to be done. There were moments when I acted as if my business challenges and fears did not exist; it provided me with some temporary sanity, but of course, that meant the work kept piling up. On a day when the dumpster was empty, I would have thrown the whole business away if I could have, just to gain some peace. Fear gripped me in such a way that it was a consuming fire burning inside.

Thoughts of being a failure motivated me to transition out of the struggling business. I knew not everything would fall into place just by thinking happy thoughts alone. This circumstance required some action and an aggressive plan that consisted of maxing out one location while working to transition out of the struggling location.

Pride

What will members of the community think?

Pride kept me from admitting it may have been time to close the underperforming location. I cared so much about others' opinions and did not want to admit defeat. Eventually, I acknowledged that I had a serious pride issue and needed to redirect my focus. If I let go of pride, I could let go of an operation holding me back from pursuing something greater. It had run its course, and now it was time for me to run mine.

Identity

Who am I without the business?

The business had taken over my life and I had lost the true essence of who I was. I failed to realize there was so much more to life than the company. Entering the family business at the age of eighteen, never really allowed me to enjoy life. Everything was about business.

I had been in survival mode for the last five years, and it had me in a time warp trapped by mediocrity. I was unhappy and was doing just enough to get by. The business was stagnant, I was stagnant, and we were merely growing in age.

In time, I learned to silence my thoughts and the cares of the world, and I heard and felt the misery within my soul.

The Voice of the Critic

at y chi pho bi a – the abnormal and persistent fear of failure, to the degree it has negative effects on the pattern of one's life.

What ways are you managing business fears?

List three things you fear about your business.

1._____

2._____

3._____

FACE YOUR FEARS

SITUATION #1

What is the least that can happen?

What is the worst that can happen?

How will the situation impact your business?

How will the situation directly affect you?

What is your plan B?

1. (Specific) What is your new goal?

2. (Measurable) How will you track your progress?

3. (Attainable) Is this goal achievable/realistic?

4. (Relevant) Is this goal relevant to your business/business needs?

5. (Time-bound) What is the time frame to achieve this goal?

List three to six action steps that need to be taken.

1._____

2._____

3._____

4._____

5._____

6._____

SITUATION #2

What is the least that can happen?

What is the worst that can happen?

How will the situation impact your business?

How will the situation directly affect you?

THE VOICE OF THE CRITIC

What is your plan B?

6. (Specific) What is your new goal?

7. (Measurable) How will you track your progress?

8. (Attainable) Is this goal achievable/realistic?

9. (Relevant) Is this goal relevant to your business/business needs?

10. (Time-bound) What is the time frame to achieve this goal?

List three to six action steps that need to be taken.

1._____

2._____

3._____

4._____

5._____

6._____

SITUATION #3

What is the least that can happen?

What is the worst that can happen?

THE VOICE OF THE CRITIC

How will the situation impact your business?

How will the situation directly affect you?

What is your plan B?

11. (Specific) What is your new goal?

12. (Measurable) How will you track your progress?

13. (Attainable) Is this goal achievable/realistic?

14. (Relevant) Is this goal relevant to your business/business needs?

15. (Time-bound) What is the time frame to achieve this goal?

List three to six action steps that need to be taken.

1._____

2._____

3._____

4._____

5._____

6._____

CHAPTER 5

IDENTITY

If you really have your own identity, you'll keep on doing what you think is really right for you, and you'll also understand the next step you want to take.

—Helmut Lang

Do you feel as if you have lost yourself in your daily routine? Are you feeling afraid to venture beyond your nice comfortable box? If my business could talk, it would have asked, *Who has time for fun and mindless hobbies?* My entrepreneurial journey had become a thief, stealing my time and focus away from the rest of my life.

What would a thief need to do if he wanted to continue to steal from you without getting caught? The thief would have to keep you from realizing you were being robbed. Caught up in the monotony, I unknowingly forfeited my true identity.

In the month of September, a year after the fire and the flood, I was meeting with Nick Demske, the county supervisor, over coffee to discuss a youth project. During the meeting, he asked, "LaToya what do you like to do for fun?" I thought, *What a loaded question he is asking.*

In that moment, if time could have slowed down and reversed, I would have found myself a few years back sitting at the dinner table. I was working on an assignment for my life coaching certification. There were three overwhelming questions any other person may have found quite simple: what do you do for fun, what are your hobbies, and what do you enjoy doing in your spare time? While pondering the questions, I heard footsteps coming up the stairs. As the sound came closer to the top, I blurted the questions in frustration to my husband Shaun. "Don't you think these are crazy questions? Who has time for fun?"

He replied, "I am not going to agree to that. The questions sound pretty simple to me; just write down your answers." As if I had not suffered enough, he hurled the questions back at me. "What do you do for fun? What do you do in your spare time? And what are your hobbies?"

Shaun and I have this terrible habit of answering a question with a question, so we went around in circles a few times.

"What do I like to do for fun? Does anything stand out to you as far as hobbies? And what exactly do you see me doing in my spare time?" I asked.

This conversation lasted long enough to make a fresh pot of coffee. Shaun was taking his first sip. He paused and responded with a snarky tone, "It sounds to me like you really need to spend some time getting to know yourself." Then he walked away.

In that moment I realized that my life had been overshadowed by my business, and I had lost the true essence of my being.

Fast-forward seven years to my conversation with the county supervisor, patiently waiting for a response. I thought to myself, *Just be honest*. Stumbling to respond, I took a deep breath and answered, "I'm still trying to figure me out."

Wow! I just admitted to a major personal flaw, and it was so liberating. I was excited at being honest with not only him but myself. Again, the three questions challenged me to face my reality.

This time I was more accepting of the fact that somewhere along my entrepreneurial journey, I had lost control.

This would be a good time to pause and think about whether you are consumed by your business. Later, we will explore the darker side of growing complacent and not taking time for yourself.

Are You Becoming a Well-Oiled Machine?

I embraced the ideology that my business should run like a well-oiled machine. As I aggressively moved the business from infancy stage, I somehow ended up stuck in the day-to-day routine. The concept of a well-oiled machine is arriving to where the business can operate without you. Developing productive teams, systems, processes, and procedures allows you to work more on growing the business rather than getting caught up in the daily running of the business.

Somehow, I missed the point and went into overdrive. When I was not responding to internal and external crises, my mind was running, thinking of all the things that needed to be completed. To ensure that nothing escaped my memory, I kept a backup list on my phone. Just in case the phone malfunctioned, I made notes on the back of junk mail. Careful not to lose focus, I disengaged from anything beyond business to manage all the moving parts.

In my pursuit of achieving success, there was no time for breaks or small talk, which resulted in mental, emotional, and physical exertion. Like a cyborg, I was willing to self-terminate to achieve my business goals. Eventually I began to see a dark side to my determination—I was a hostage, and my business was my captor.

Over the years, a few individuals expressed a genuine concern that I was growing stagnant. On a Friday afternoon I was visited by Dr. Jaqueline Love. A mutual friend connected us and thought we could collaborate on a project. As we went through the motions of sharing information about our programs, passions, and career paths, we instantly clicked. After several phone calls, lunches, and pop-in visits, she finally said something that left me with mixed emotions.

"You have done a great job building your establishment," she began. "I hope you do not take offense to this, but you are so much bigger than what you are currently doing. There is much more for you to do beyond this. Do you have an exit strategy? I mean, what's next after this?"

I took the remark as an insult as my small thinking kept me from seeing anything else beyond business. How dare she even suggest there was anything beyond what I had worked so hard to create? I had navigated my way through various positions, and I had finally made it. In my mind, the business and I were one; there was no separation even if I had achieved all my goals. It would be a betrayal for me to consider otherwise.

I was stuck in such a limited mindset that I failed to realize she was speaking to my potential. I later realized my happiness and identity were being sacrificed, and I was a mere extension of the business. I was hanging on to the business just to hang on and had lost my innovation, creativity, and entrepreneurial spirit. The conversation with Jacqueline made me realize that my business had become my idol and was stunting my growth.

I eventually discovered that sometimes letting go is essential to your continuous growth, development, and freedom.

Are You Being Held Hostage?

It is easy to get lost in the hustle and bustle as you work your way through growing and sustaining your business. To maintain a clear focus, you must learn to step away. Stepping away will allow you to identify how much time you are working *in* the business compared to how much time you are working *on* the business. You must make sure you don't cross that line from dedication to obsession, and risk losing yourself to your business.

Let's talk about those mindless hobbies. Although I am still on my path to finding what I enjoy, hobbies are a great way to disconnect. The aim is that you let go of your conveyor-belt responsibilities and find joy in your personal life. No one wants to work for a machine; it is the great personalities of entrepreneurs that make employees want to work for them. Find what hobbies bring you joy, and that happiness will be apparent in the rest of your life.

It's also important not to lose your professional identity outside of your current venture. Failure to acknowledge your skills, abilities, and potential will most likely prevent you from accepting and seeking new challenges. This lack of vision will put you in a place of stagnation, and you and your business will both stop growing.

Take a moment to pause and gather your thoughts. What are you thinking? Do you know where those thoughts are coming from? Have you considered whether your thoughts are coming from fear of what people might say or think? As a visionary, I have always had a rather exceptional ability to paint pictures in my mind. As I wrestled with the idea of releasing the struggling location, I visualized images of an abandoned building with people peering in the windows giving their version of what they thought went wrong. As those images haunted me, I chose to hold on tighter out of fear of the others' opinions. My decision to carry on cost me many nights of peaceful sleep. It all boiled down to having an issue of pride and proving to my family, friends, and community I was a success.

Now is a good time to stop and think about whether you are being held captive.

Identity

Do you find yourself in either of the two conversations that occur with Shaun and the county supervisor?

What would have been your responses?

What do you like to do for fun?

What are your hobbies?

What do you like to do in your spare time?

IDENTITY

Concerning Jacqueline, how would you have responded to her suggestion that you were greater than your business?

Do you have any goals beyond operating a business? If so, what?

In what way (if at all) has the business had an impact on your identity?

Do you feel you have lost who you truly are to your business?

In what way do you feel you may have lost your identity to your business?

CHAPTER 6

TICKING TIME BOMB

Pessimism may support the realism we so often need.
—Martin E.P. Seligman

Taking over the family business appeared to be the perfect Cinderella story. It was all that I had ever dreamed of, and I could not imagine it any other way. However, stress and pressure to sustain a business during an economic crisis, seasons of underperformance, and wavering employees was often overwhelming. At some point, I found it a challenge to slow down my thoughts, and my constant worry was interfering with my ability to sleep through the night. I was so overwhelmed with mental lists of new ideas and overlooked tasks that I eventually began keeping a journal on my nightstand. It never failed that by the next morning I would have a full page of scribbled notes.

I had convinced myself that multitasking was one of my greatest strengths. I quickly learned how to maneuver through this entrepreneurial lifestyle: I completed work tasks as more piled up, I attended multiple business engagements and covered shifts when needed, and that required that I work late every night. My mind was on autopilot, and without realizing it I reached a level of burnout several times but unfortunately ignored the signs until I ultimately crashed. Sadly, the expectations that I had for myself I required of others. Unfortunately, this led to employee burnout, which had a negative impact on the business.

In interviewing entrepreneurs for my research study, I discovered that many entrepreneurs push themselves to a point of burnout due to the feelings of guilt, anxiety, and uncertainty. In the rest of this chapter, I will use my personal experiences to demonstrate how each feeling can contribute to your ticking time bomb.

Guilt

My feelings of guilt were rooted in the idea of letting go.

I felt guilty for doing anything beyond business for myself and kept moving, ignoring my personal needs, such as managing my stress level. Unaware of the negative effect this was having on me, I kept ticking like a time bomb ready to explode at any moment. To me, business success meant running nonstop to complete all demands. My feelings of guilt were rooted in meeting high expectations and my fundamental belief that quitting was not an option.

To stay true to my roots, I never considered that stepping back from the business a bit could be good for my mental health. As a third-generation entrepreneur, I felt the need to keep pushing. In the moments I got tired I could hear the words of my father, "You only have a small time frame to grow the business as much as you can to set the next generation up. That window of opportunity closes quickly; run as fast as you can." In my mind, running as fast as you can meant that there were no moments for slowing down or sitting down. The thought alone of taking a break, resting, or letting go bought forth so much guilt.

I poured my time, energy, and love into my business, and in return it was slowly suffocating me. My loyalty to the business and pride kept me from seeing the betrayal—my business was not offering me peace of mind as it should. I eventually accepted that while I was giving my all, I would not receive the entrepreneurial freedom that everyone talked about. The hope of financial stability and freedom that came with being an entrepreneur quickly diminished, but I felt I was in too deep. As I continued down this path, I questioned whether things would ever change for the better. When things got too overwhelming, thoughts of closing the business rippled through my mind. Looking for a way to escape the anxiety, I made bold announcements to my father that I was shutting it all down, yet I continued to stay because it was all I had ever known.

A constant accumulation of stress and pressure over time can lead to burnout. It is important to take notice of prolonged emotional, physical, and mental exhaustion. Your possible feelings of guilt may have pushed you beyond what you can withstand physically, emotionally, or mentally. The fear of being a quitter—and even possibly a failure—is what will guilt-trip you into taking further action and remain in a hostage situation. There is an unhealthy commitment to remain loyal to your business no matter the cost. Staying without a desire to remain, however, can create feelings of resentment and bitterness.

Anxiety

In 2010, during the economic crisis, the childcare facilities had been battle-tested financially, and the business was struggling to survive. Each week was a struggle to meet payroll and taxes while trying to maintain staff and clients. Consistent challenges eventually shaped my mind into always expecting the worse. At times, the opposition was so great I was unaware of whether we would find a way out.

As I settled into a mindset of stinking thinking, anxiety and panic attacks became my norm. I became a pro at constantly worrying when the next disaster would strike but still finding a solution every

TICKING TIME BOMB

time. Although every situation always worked out, my anxiety took a toll on my mental health, and I began lashing out at my employees.

I remember an incident where Rachel, the accounts payable clerk worked aggressively to resolve a financial matter. She was on a roll with researching information while gathering data for a report that was due to one of our stakeholders. In an effort to inform me of the necessary documentation needed, Rachel sent out a text message that read, "I will need the following information ASAP." I immediately stopped reading the text as I immediately felt myself growing irritable.

Tick! Tick! Tick! Tick! ... BOOM!

My heart raced. I felt myself trembling and my chest tightening. I paced the floor, tried to gather my thoughts. *How would I confront the clerk? She should have requested additional time to gather the information!*

Initially, I started to send a text but was in so much distress that I picked up the phone and called her. After about fifteen minutes of me going on and on about not receiving sufficient notice, she responded, "It was nothing that you needed to stop and do at the moment. It was just something that we need to get done as soon as possible, but I didn't mean for you to literally stop what you were doing."

After taking a moment to breathe and calm down, I questioned how I reacted. I decided to take a walk as I recounted what occurred. Eventually, I picked up my phone and went back to my message. There it was boldly, in plain sight: "ASAP." I felt triggered by that word. I interpreted it to mean, *LaToya, stop working on what you are doing now and address this immediately.* I was already under stress and pressure from going back and forth with the insurance company. I had been working on a business loss income report that was holding up our business loss payout. This report was the answer to covering payroll and taxes, and now I had more weight added to my shoulders. The load I was carrying was heavy. Out of fear of failing to complete everything and not meet financial obligations, I snapped under pressure.

I was living in a constant state of anxiety and had succumbed to fear. That was not the first time my anxiety got the better of me, and it would not be the last. My mind had been trained to expect a crisis anytime the phone rang before seven a.m.

In February 2015, at 6:10 a.m., my phone shrieked like a fire alarm pulled in an emergency. I knew it must be something urgent when I saw the center director's name, Natasha, scrolling across my screen. Either she was experiencing something personally, or it was a business situation. Whatever it was, it needed my immediate attention. I cleared my throat and searched for a lively tone as I answered.

"Toya, we have a serious issue," said Natasha.

"Okay, shoot!" I responded.

In a hurried voice, Natasha explained that when she arrived at the building, there was a notice posted on the front door from the electric company. There had been a fire and a flood Sunday evening. It had been an unseasonably warm day, and ice from the rooftop melted and somehow seeped into the circuit breaker, causing a fire in the kitchen. As a result, the sprinkler system was triggered, causing a flood. Immediately my stress level pushed me out of bed and anxiety gripped my focus once again.

Uncertainty

Feelings of uncertainty can come in many different sizes and situations. It may be stress from a disastrous situation you have never experienced, or it may form as doubt in making the next big decision. It could even mean being uncertain of the bigger picture when you find yourself asking, *Is this the life I want? Is this business right for me?*

Natasha's phone call left me in a state of uncertainty, and I did not know if this new challenge would force me to close the location. I had been feeling as though it was possibly time to let go, and in that moment, I was afraid that we might not survive this challenge. I sprang into action, jumped out of bed, quickly got myself ready, and ran out the door. From the sound of it, a lot of work would need to be done. For now, my focus was getting to the center so I could assess the damage. I needed to get a grip on what we were up against. I had no idea what to expect, but visions of a charred building with water-stained walls ran wild through my mind.

As I continued to replay the phone call in my mind, my imagination kept creating images each more vivid and horrific than the next. I never thought there would be a time when my creative problem-solving skills would fail me. Being in unknown territory, I had to take a few moments to talk myself off the ledge. I kept repeating variations of "LaToya, just relax; you'll learn the extent of the damage when you get there. Come on, keep it together; you were built for this."

Encouraging myself worked for about three minutes, then my mind ran rampant again. *Who should I call? What needs to be done first? How long will we have to stay closed? Will the insurance cover everything?*

I finally arrived at the scene. I felt like I was walking into an intensive care unit, fearing the condition I would find a loved one in. As I entered, I quickly noticed the wet carpet; however, there was no charred equipment, water-stained walls, or anything like I originally envisioned. I made my way to the rear of the building, where the fire had started. When I had heard over the phone the explanation of what occurred, it just sounded like it was going to be a nightmare. It was nothing like I expected and appeared to be more smoke and water damage. The cosmetic repairs led me to believe that we would be back up and running in no time.

Three days later, the insurance adjuster finally arrived, walking through the building with his clipboard in hand. As he reviewed each room, he documented his findings in silence. The only sound I heard was the clicking of the pen.

I was losing my patience. I wanted to yank the pen from his hand and yell, *What is it?* I thought, *Is the silence an indication there is not much to repair, or does it suggest something beyond what we could see?*

"So, the building has just been sitting for three days, huh," he finally said, clearly more of a statement than a question.

I thought, *Well, of course, where else would it go?* but instead replied with a simple yes.

He told us there needed to be heat restored to the building as soon as possible, or mold would set in within a matter of days. To our surprise, the heating unit on the rooftop had been destroyed. The repairs and replacement would require the work of both the electric company and an electrician. My insurance would most likely cover it and then go after the property owner's insurance; however, we would have to pay the upfront cost and then wait to be reimbursed.

The insurance adjuster made it clear: either make the repairs now or risk the accumulation of additional damages, for which I would be held liable. I realized the damage was worse than I had anticipated, and this location would not be back open in no time.

After contacting an electrician referred by the insurance agent, we discovered it would cost thousands of dollars. We could not afford to fork out that kind of money; I had payroll and taxes that needed to be covered. During 2009 to 2010, the business experienced financial challenges, and I had just established a payment agreement with the Internal Revenue Service. We did not have the funds for an electrician. I suggested that we wait to hear from the property owner.

The feeling of uncertainty was at the helm, and I was unsure of what to do next. I felt like I was standing in a whirlwind fighting to maintain my balance. Trouble was all around me, and my inability to maintain focus only exacerbated the situation. I was waiting for my "Dorothy moment," when I would wake up to find that everything had been a dream.

But reality soon set in. I still had another operation to run while trying to make impossible decisions regarding the fire and water damage. The insurance company wanted the repairs done immediately. In contrast, the property owners wanted to know when they could expect their next rent payment. I had made the decision to consolidate staff into the primary location, much to their frustration. Clients noticed we were struggling and opted to find new providers. Both the business and my personal bank accounts were depleted while debt rapidly increased. Bank accounts were running negative on Monday while payroll and taxes were due on Friday. I paced the floor at the office, embracing the knots in my stomach, trying to figure out how I would meet payroll while Shaun sent text messages: "What's for dinner babe?" "What time will you be home?"

Shaun loved cooking, which was one of the many ways he expressed his love to our family. However, he greatly desired that I contribute ideas to the meal planning so that once he got home from work, things would run more smoothly at the home front. When I finally made it home, there was a sink full of dishes left from dinner, a cold plate of dinner in the microwave, and an assignment needing to be completed in Blackboard. As my daughters shared the highlights of their day, I noticed the mail sitting on the table. My mind seemed to drift as the girls continued to narrate their day with dramatic sound effects and hand motions. I could not seem to stay focused.

The Ripple Effect

I questioned whether we would ever reopen. During the renovation process, the team worked hard to maximize clients at the location still in operation. Their efforts proved to be a success. Although our client base was increasing, the team was chaotic and falling apart.

Consolidating the two teams proved a greater challenge than I realized. Since both teams followed the same policy, processes, and procedures at their separate facilities, I figured the consolidation would be a simple transition. *What could have possibly gone wrong?*

I eventually discovered what was contributing to the loss of morale. I consolidated the two facilities with promises of it being a temporary solution, but I could not maintain the positive energy while trying to cope with all the negative thoughts and challenges I was experiencing. Despite the employees' clear frustrations, I got comfortable with everyone being under one roof while I worked through the challenges.

Another issue I overlooked was the work culture; I should have considered the two facilities had different environments. Even though the policies and procedures were the same, the operations had unique rhythms. It became a game of tug-of-war with both teams fighting for power. Eventually I lost a great administrator who was uniquely trained for the position. Mel had a unique skillset that the rest of the management team did not possess, and her departure had a significant impact on the business.

The task list continued to grow, and issues continued to arise. We were losing valuable staff but still had payroll for the excess of employees working in a single location. We had less money coming in, and I soon learned the insurance payout for loss of income would not be nearly as much as I had anticipated.

To my surprise, I learned the business was underinsured, which resulted in a penalty and only 40 percent of the estimated payout. I had no idea how this could have happened; each year we reported annual revenue, square footage, and the number of employees to our insurance company to renew the policy. How could the company servicing the business for the last two years not have a grip on the business income? I was angry, frustrated, and worried all at the same time, but I was aware I had to take some ownership for the mistake—as a business owner I should have reviewed the policy more closely.

I was grateful for my accountant's support at this time. Serving our family for about twenty years, Liz thrived in a crisis and was always up for a challenge. We compiled a list of concerns and prepared for a great debate. As I prepared to make a call to the agency, I received an email from the insurance adjuster, stating that since the repairs were made, we were expected to immediately move back into the facility and work towards recovering the business. The insurance agency made it clear that we needed to get back to where we were financially prior to the fire.

My reaction: *Wow! Wow! Wow!*

What took ten years to build my insurance company was expecting me to recover in two weeks.

My time bomb was ticking away, and I didn't know how much more I could take on my own. I had committed myself to prayer, submitted prayer requests, but my faith was constantly shaken. I felt like I was under attack and had no one to talk to about my experiences. Every day it was something different occurring, and it was weighing heavily on me. Feeling as though my family and friends did not understand, I retreated and suffered silently.

I was trying to create and execute my plan of action while coping with the stress and pressure to perform while writing a dissertation on the entrepreneurial experience of business loss. Needless to say, I could not seem to stay focused, and I definitely didn't want to receive any more of Shaun's what's-for-dinner-babe texts. I was not in control of my life, and I felt like the business was holding me hostage.

Are You Being Held Hostage?

Losing control and not knowing what will occur next can be frightening. Feelings of uncertainty and anxiety present many barriers and challenges that interfere with your ability to maintain focus during business challenges. As you try to get a grip on a variety of emotions, you fight hard to maintain control of yourself. The business can become a stronghold gripping and controlling how you respond and react to situations. You can become a ticking time bomb as you stand on guard waiting for the next catastrophe.

As I continued to work my way through the many obstacles, I wrestled with the idea of letting it all go. As I reevaluated my life and refocused my thoughts, I felt as though an exodus was the best for me. However, if my business could talk, it would have asked, *What about all the people—do you want them to see you fail?*

Time Bomb

List six major business struggles that you have encountered over the last six months. How have they impacted you?

Business Challenges	How have they impacted you?
Inability to meet payroll	Loss of appetite and sleep worrying about how I would pay individuals.

Do you find that your business is providing the expected financial return? _____

If yes, when do you anticipate seeing that return?

☐ 6 months ☐ 12 months ☐ 18 months ☐ 24 months

If no, why do you continue to hold on?

TICKING TIME BOMB

In working to continue to achieve those results, do you feel you will be negatively affected in any of the following ways?

- ☐ Physically
- ☐ Mentally
- ☐ Emotionally
- ☐ Financially

If you had to choose one area you would risk for your business to succeed, what area would it be?

- ☐ Personal finances
- ☐ Emotional well-being
- ☐ Physical health
- ☐ Mental health
- ☐ None of the above

How are you managing your challenges? Choose one answer below.

- ☐ I am managing my challenges independently and I feel like I can continue managing them independently.
- ☐ I am managing them independently but feel as though I need additional support.
- ☐ My support network includes family and friends.
- ☐ I do not have a support network.

Complete the following: Research and identify a business coach and mental health counselor (List names and contact information below).

	Name & Contact Information:
Business Coach	
Mental Health Counselor	

CHAPTER 7

FIND YOUR MOMENT OF MEANING

You must first be who you really are, then do what you need to do, in order to have what you want.

—Margaret Young

My morning routine included showering and throwing on a T-shirt and jeans. The days were unpredictable and lacked a sense of stability. I made sure to dress comfortably. I never knew what I would be challenged by; I just had to be ready.

I anxiously waited for responses from the insurance company and property owners while closely monitoring the finances. The temporary closure for repairs drained the business financially. The constant stress took its toll on my body, and I had moments where I entered what I call the zone, a place where my eyes became fixated on the computer, but dazed. Within a matter of minutes, I was lost in my thoughts, my body became numb, and it felt like I was paralyzed. Through the years, I had learned to pull myself out of the zone when I felt myself slipping away. I found comfort in prayer. My faith in overcoming my trials and circumstances was made stronger as I meditated on the Word of God.

It was another typical day at the office, and I had worked up enough courage to schedule a meeting with my commercial loan officer for financial support. While I gathered my belongings, my keys fell to the floor. I suddenly noticed my dingy, paint-splattered, black-and-white Chuck Taylors. I took one look in the mirror and noticed that I was wearing a bleach-stained T-shirt and wrinkled jeans, accented by my signature low ponytail and bangs swooped to the side.

LaToya, you look a hot mess. Where are you going looking like that? At this point it was not about people pleasing; it was that I was not looking at the LaToya I once knew. I had purchased a commercial property eight years before the fire, and I remembered the loan officer looking at me seriously and saying, "Kid, this is a great business plan you have put together. I want you to know that it's not the plan I believe in, it is you."

After replaying his words in my mind, I knew that I needed to pull myself together. It was in that moment that I remembered who I was—an amazing visionary with an exceptional ability to strategically create plans. I was not only able to create them, but I knew I was great at selling my idea and plans as well. This reflection is just what I needed to walk into the bank confidently and professionally, a businesswoman asking for assistance in executing a plan. I went home and transformed and took a moment to breathe and encourage myself. *God, I know you got me. LaToya, let's do this.*

I swung open the car door at the bank and stepped out with a winning attitude, wearing my black heels, designer jeans, and blazer accented with pearls. It had been a while, and the click of my heels was giving me life as I reclaimed my confidence. Upon entering the bank, I greeted the receptionist with a triumphant smile.

Negotiating

"Come on in, LaToya," the banker said.

Walking into his office with my head held high and my purse strap slung over my shoulder, I extended my hand for a handshake.

"It has been a while," I said. "Thanks for allowing me to come in at such short notice."

"Of course, LaToya, that's why I'm here," he said. "How can we help you today?"

With his notepad positioned in front of him, he grabbed an ink pen out of the caddy on his desk.

"We have a situation," I began. "There was a fire and a flood at one of the locations. After enjoying that unseasonably warm weather, the ice melted and somehow seeped into the circuit breaker causing a fire and a flood."

"Wow! That's horrible, LaToya!"

I quickly assured him that the fire did not occur at the location for which we had secured the loan, but at the property we were leasing.

"It has been a headache getting the repairs moving, but we do have a plan," I said.

"Okay, great! What are the plans?"

"I plan to consolidate temporarily," I explained. "We will be offering transportation services to our clients interested in utilizing our alternate location less than thirty miles away. I figured this would allow us to maintain some of our clients. However, I realize not all of them may be comfortable using services outside of their county. Also, our employees will commute to this location, so we are fully staffed. This will take us time because we are trying to execute a smooth transition, but I am confident that it will work."

"Sounds like a good plan," he agreed. "I like the idea of transferring your clients. So how can I help?"

"I need you to consider deferring the commercial loan for ninety days. That would provide us with some financial relief."

He wrote "defer loan payments" on his notepad.

"We also have a payroll this Friday, and I am concerned about that. Is there any way you will allow a pass-through of funds? With everything going on, I want to make sure the payroll is covered. Also, I would like to request a line of credit."

"Okay, got it," he responded. "Let me crunch some numbers and see what we can do, LaToya."

Within a couple of days, I received a call that the loan was modified, the line of credit added, and the bank agreed to cover payroll.

Learning to cope with difficult emotions while balancing work and home life can be exhausting. The constant struggle without a clear vision of where you are heading may have you in a desolate place mentally. Trust me, you will find your way out. First, however, you must find the strength to reclaim your identity. The key to staying free requires that you discover who you are without the weight and pressure that so easily entrapped you. The confidence and courage that allowed you to start or take over the business still lies within, and you must regain your strength. Realizing who you are, and not what this situation has forced you to become, is essential to your growth.

My moment of meaning was coming to the point of putting pride aside to ask for help for the sake of my emotional well-being and the company. My faith and belief that things would change would not be activated until I took action. However, I first had to acknowledge that I needed help and that needing help didn't mean I was less of a person. I had to come to the end of myself and recognize that I'd had some really great seasons, but I was in a place where I needed assistance. Moreover, I had to come to a place where I recognized I was not alone in my struggles. Once I put my ego aside and came to the end of myself, I was then able to not only see what needed to be done but move confidently in doing what needed to be done.

Your Moment of Meaning

List five of your strengths.

1._____

2._____

3._____

4._____

5._____

Now visit this website and complete the Clifton Strengths Talent Assessment: https://www.gallup.com/cliftonstrengths/en/252137/home.aspx

List the top five strengths identified:

1._____

2._____

3._____

4._____

5._____

Do you agree with the results? Why or why not?

CHAPTER 8

ESCAPE PLAN

For tomorrow belongs to the people who prepare for it today.
—African Proverb

Deciding to step outside your comfort zone is bravery. The daily hustle and routine limits the fear of the unknown; however, it increases your chances of slipping into a place of stagnation. There is a freedom in comfort that knows no strain or struggle. Eventually, I found myself in a place of unfruitfulness. As long as I kept the routine constant, there would be no challenges or risk. Initially, letting go for me appeared to have many challenges and risks. The most logical thing to do would have been to exchange my daily routine for executing an exit plan. However, I struggled with letting go for a peculiar reason—I had grown comfortable working in chaos. I no longer had vision, and I was content with being a taskmaster and a fire extinguisher. Finding my way out meant journeying into unfamiliar territory to face new challenges.

The evolution of you takes bravery as you exchange familiarity for the unknown. Journeying into new territory can leave you feeling overwhelmed but offers new opportunities while discovering the new and improved you.

I had been moving full speed ahead and had failed to notice my discontent. The business was my main priority, and my family was on the back burner. They continued to wait for the perfect moment where they would have my undivided attention. But I was always distracted by negative thoughts and stood on guard waiting for the next crisis. My phone became a constant companion even during the most intimate moments with my husband. Explosive arguments preceded vacations due to my irritability stemming from the unknown.

My loving husband now demanded that I relinquish the business because of the physical and mental toll it was having on my life. He felt that the business had control over me and that I was neglecting the family. In my opinion, he was failing to acknowledge the legacy I had been working hard to grow to benefit the family. In reality, I failed to consider his opinions and created smoke and mirrors and kept running in circles. Later, I realized that he only wanted me to reclaim my life.

Realization consumed me in the midnight hours, haunting me like the Ghost of Christmas Past, bringing anxiety, uncertainty, and fear. The days of living in my head and running nonstop interfered with me coming to the point of realizing that perhaps I had lost control of my life. My emotions were at the helm guiding my thoughts and behavior, and I had lost control. The progress I made was an emotional quick fix that distracted me from being free.

After financial relief came from the bank, and a path out of this disaster finally emerged, I could admit to myself that I was not fighting to save my business but my own ego and reputation.

When I acknowledged that my loss was an experience and did not define me, anxiety, uncertainty, and fear were immediately cut down to size. As I regained control, the horizon became so much clearer. This experience presented two new exciting opportunities: I could use my skills and talents to rebuild the organization, or I could create a new path.

A change of focus will allow you to assess your emotions, thoughts, and experience. Choosing to refocus also provides an opportunity to learn from your experience. You can learn from your experience by carefully examining and assessing the root issues of your challenges and how you managed them.

Once you have come to a point of realization and have spent some time evaluating your experience, you can then refocus. The period of refocusing will look different for everyone. However, it most likely will include an exit and a brief or extended pause to rediscover the new and improved you and what your new journey will entail.

Your period of refocusing will eventually lead you to a point of relaunching. This can be both frightening and exciting. Relaunching could include a renewed focus that implements a new and improved business plan that strengthens your current business. On the other hand, you may consider launching a new business idea while implementing your newfound knowledge and experiences. For some, relaunching may include avoiding entrepreneurship in exchange for a new career path. This process is evolutionary and a redefining moment as you use the knowledge gained from your experience to catapult you into your new journey.

In developing my published qualitative research study for my dissertation, "The Entrepreneurial Experience of Business Loss," I used Kurt Lewin's (1958) changed model as a theoretical framework in developing what I identify as the 3R Redemptive Model. Lewin's change model is initiated by three steps: unfreezing, changing and refreezing.

Unfreeze → Change → Refreeze

The initial step of unfreezing creates a consciousness that change is necessary. The second step involves moving toward a preferred level of change, while the final step involves instituting the new change. Unfreezing allows you to evaluate your mindset and business processes that may not be working. As you come to a point of realization, you accept that change is imperative. This new insight allows you to refocus and make the changes that will thrust you to your next destination. Finally, the refreezing stage requires that you relaunch into what you have identified as your new normal.

In the next three chapters, I offer a similar model to Lewin's. Where Lewin focuses on managerial functions that need to change within an organization, this model focuses on the entrepreneurial mindset that needs to change in time of crisis: Realization, Refocus, and Relaunch. This model takes more of a personal approach to determining where you may be stuck and how to move beyond that place.

Realization → Refocus → Relaunch

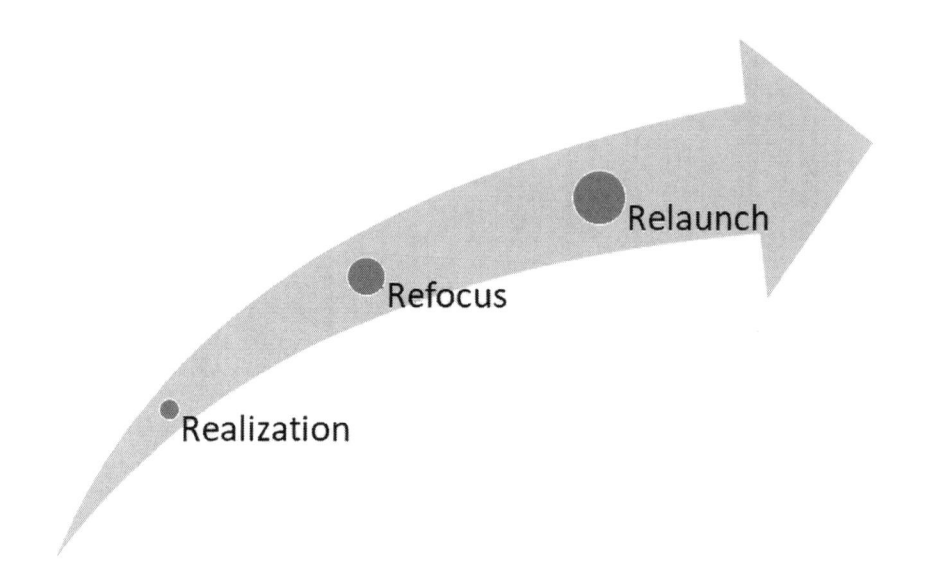

Escape Plan

REALIZATION

Carefully evaluate the performance of your business. What are the challenges? How does that directly impact the business?

REFOCUS

What areas should you adjust?

What task needs to be completed to make that adjustment?

What information needs to be researched?

RELAUNCH

What do you see as your new normal?

What steps should you take to get to that new normal?

What are ways to introduce your new normal to the world?

CHAPTER 9

REALIZATION

Realization encourages a concentrated effort to pick up the pieces so you can progress beyond emotional distress.
—LaToya Thurmond

Let's begin by defining what this term really means:

> **re al i za tion** – an act of becoming *fully aware* of something as a fact [emphasis added][3]

Realization brought me to a point of removing the blindfold so I could see my reality. That included recognizing and admitting that I was the real captor. I had been unwilling to let go of a business that I needed to release. As I continued to battle with negative emotions and the self-inflicted pressure to continue, I gripped my business and held on tight. Eventually I realized that I possessed the power to choose whether I maintained or discontinued the operation.

---

[3] Realization. Definition from Google, provided by Oxford Languages.

Step 1: Realize the Need for Change

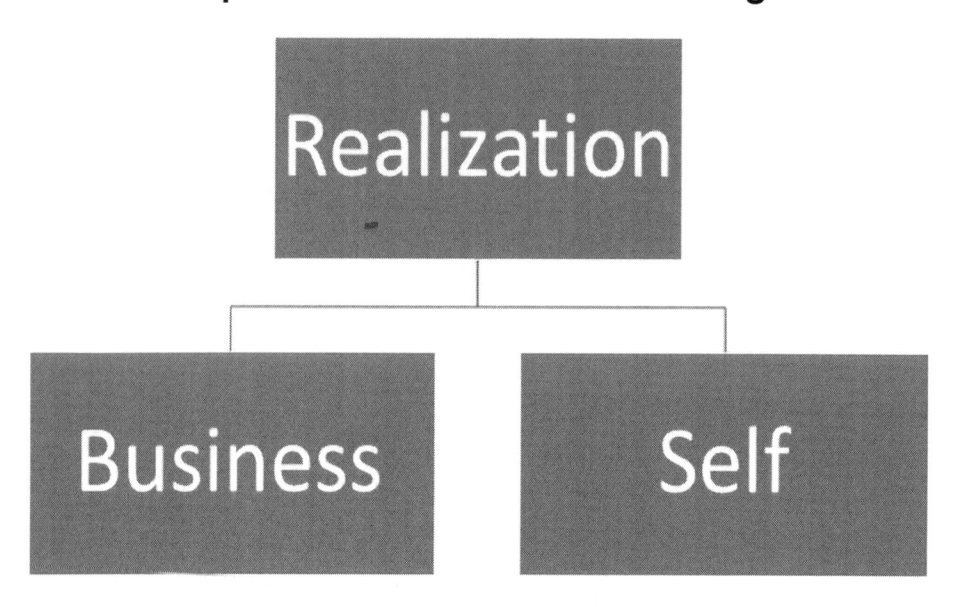

```
        ┌──────────────┐
        │ Realization  │
        └──────┬───────┘
         ┌─────┴─────┐
    ┌────┴────┐ ┌────┴────┐
    │ Business│ │  Self   │
    └─────────┘ └─────────┘
```

Recognize the Need for Business Change

I realize how tough this can be. At one point, your business was like a newborn, and you were excited to welcome it to the world. You imagined all the ways it would change the world, and you would give your all to see it come to fruition. As your business continued to develop, you were pleased by its progress, or you had concerns. You may have even noticed that it needed your extra attention throughout the years. You may have found it was advancing and blossoming beyond what you had imagined. If you have experienced anything like I have, you may have even viewed your business as a testy teenager. I paced the floor nightly worried about its well-being, and I shed many tears. When you have invested, nurtured, and worked hard to develop your business, it's hard to let go.

Being honest with myself required that I first commit to answering some tough questions.

1. What is your ultimate business goal?
2. Have you achieved that goal?
3. Does the business have the potential to advance?
4. Do you have the necessary skills needed to take it to its next level of advancement?
5. If you have the skills to take it to the next level, how much time are you committed to its advancement?
6. If you don't have the skills needed, what are your plans?

My truth was that I did not know if I had the skills to take it to a new level. Why? Because I did not know what that next level was. That is why I cannot stress enough the importance of having a clear vision and following a solid business and exit plan.

In my situation, I could have created a recovery and growth strategy. After completing the plan, I would have had to work through determining if I had what it took to get the business to that new destination. Perhaps I could have even prepared a successor or arranged to sell the business.

After taking some time to be brutally honest with myself, I realized that I just did not want to continue. I had no desire to develop a strategy, plan, or build a new team. Once I arrived at a place of being okay with what I wanted, I quickly found my exit. For years my thoughts had been in total control of my actions. Once I changed my thoughts, my actions changed, and I saw why it was so important for me to let go.

Eventually, I saw clearly how I had lost sight of the fact that letting go of one location would not be the end of the legacy. The threat to the legacy was the struggling location and my maladaptive behavior.

Self

Eventually I realized that the business had run its course and that I had not failed. I felt a sense of freedom just arriving at this new place of understanding. You can discover the unseen benefit of letting go. It all boils down to realization, which requires that you first self-evaluate. There is liberation in recognizing that the state of your business does not define your identity or success. Having a fresh new start is exciting and refreshing. According to research, failure has a way of stimulating the development of critical skills and knowledge that can be applied to new ventures (McGrath, 1999; Minniti & Bygrave, 2001). Suppose you choose a fresh start in business this time around. In that case, you will be following a modified business model influenced by your entrepreneurial experience. On the other hand, the journey to freedom comes at the point of release. As a creative being, you can step out of your comfort zone to create a new path. Your experience allows you to see there is a world waiting for you to show up.

Choose to step out of your comfortable box to create a new path. Realization allows you to see your challenge as an opportunity to soar to newer heights. Coming out of your situation will be a process, but decide to believe that your usual is about to change. Once you get past your emotions, you can move forward. Seek to strengthen your mindset and acquire the power to cancel all negative thoughts. Why? Because you have a future ahead of you.

Consider This

- What do you want at this point in your life?
- Are you happy?
- Have you lost the passion and drive?
- What amount of energy are you fully committed to pouring into the business?

REALIZATION

- Do you have a vision for furthering the growth and development of your business, and if so, what does it look like?
- If you do not have a vision, then what is next?

You can no longer ignore how you feel and what you have experienced. Emotions are only for the moment and are subject to change. We can sometimes give emotions power they do not deserve. Acknowledge your emotions, but do not plan to stay there. Perhaps you are dreading the things you must do to exit your establishment. I know your task list can sound like the song that never ends, but have you considered the cost you pay if you stay in a place you no longer desire to be? Forgive yourself for the mistakes you have made.

I am here to tell you if you want out, there is a way of escape, and you can most definitely take back your control. The first thing you must do is come to the realization of whether you want to stay on the journey or discontinue. You should take time to be honest with yourself because *you* deserve it and the others walking in the wilderness alongside you do too!

Comfort came in writing my dissertation. I kept hearing the voice of one participant: "I wasn't pleased anyway. I had achieved all that I had ever set my mind to do, and I grew bored." I took a moment to reflect, and I thought about how I felt that the business was consuming me mentally and emotionally. I had overcome many business crises one after the other and never took a moment to pause. Always jumping from one fire to the next became my usual, and being stressed out was my normal.

My husband continued to question why I kept holding on. He witnessed firsthand how the organization had drained me physically, emotionally, and financially. For years I listened to what I considered to be him grumbling, all while I kept pushing right past all his wisdom and concern.

The Home Front

Shaun and the girls had extreme patience, and they were always excited to see me walk through the door. Arion was a senior in high school, and Shia was in second grade. They always had so much to share about their day. It took a long time for me to realize how I had allowed business and its many challenges to interfere with my ability to see that my daughters also were great visionaries and how extremely excited they were about their futures.

Challenges showed up daily, and I had a serious issue with not giving them attention. There were moments when we would gather in our favorite place, the kitchen. The girls and Shaun would engage in frequent giggle chats and when I did tune in I felt left out. I would ask, *Why didn't anyone tell me?* or *What did I miss?*

Shaun's response never failed. "Babe, you are always on that phone or in that computer. It is as if you are here physically, but not mentally. We are talking to you, and it is as if you cannot hear anything."

I intentionally planned mini-vacations for birthdays and anniversaries. As much as I like planning mini-vacations and packing the necessary items for our stay, I never really enjoyed myself. Most people take a vacation to relax and unwind. I on the other hand was just fascinated with the idea that we would be going somewhere—perhaps even excited about working in a different location for the weekend. Although I kept my commitment to mini-vacations and anniversary getaways, I struggled with disconnecting mentally. I always managed to pack an invisible suitcase named Work. It consisted of payroll, tax responsibilities, employee concerns, and various issues that demanded my attention.

My mind was in constant motion trying to plan and resolve issues. I was failing at being present, and I was missing so many wonderful memories. My family was coping with my constant absence while silently suffering. I had lost control and could not stop long enough to see I was not well. My mind was constantly unraveling with ideas, issues, and concerns. On the outside, it looked as if I had it all together, but people had no clue. I was fortunate to have a loving family that overlooked my shortcomings and loved me with all my flaws and inconsistencies.

Although I took a while to see the light, I eventually discovered how important it is that you do not lose yourself and your loved ones while trying to achieve success. When drowning in your work, it seems as if you are constantly holding your breath. When you are in a constant mode of survival, you are never really thinking about happiness; you are simply working to survive.

Happiness

I had to think about the word happiness for a while, and I mean a long while. I had spent so many years trying to keep the businesses alive that I sacrificed my own happiness. Honestly, I had no clue what even made me happy. Joy was having 50 percent of payroll in the bank on a Friday so if staff happened to go to the financial institution where the business banked to cash their check, they were not turned away. Delight was having no disconnects on the electric bill and definitely an empty dumpster. Pleasure was having clients who had no complaints and no state violations. Happiness was Friday night when the clock struck midnight, knowing that most likely nothing would occur on the weekend. Surviving every week became my happiness. The constant battle prevented me from thinking of the things that genuinely made me happy. Complacency had set in, and I had grown comfortable with surviving.

The miracle was that I was able to self-evaluate and see how this was weighing heavily on my family and me. My beautiful family had become comfortable with me not being present, and that was a problem. In my moments of reflection, I realized there was a miracle in the fire and flood.

I was holding on because I was afraid the organization could not survive without both locations. Time had proved that we could operate with one location, and I realized an opportunity to reduce overhead cost and stress. In my moment of reflection, I then remembered asking God one thing: "God, whenever my season is up, please allow me to bow out gracefully." Perhaps this was that moment.

The journey to your exit may seem distant; however, arriving at a point of realization brings you out of the darkness. You must do some adjusting to the light of facts while facing uncertainty. Refocusing can be intimidating once you discover all transitional tasks necessary for your departure. Nevertheless, seeing a glimpse of your future without the weight and responsibility of your business will bring much liberation.

Take Action:

1. Take a moment to think about the current condition of your business. (how is it performing; what are the challenges and barriers?).
2. Analyze the situation to identify the cause of the situation (self, poor management, tragedy, lack of skills, no longer committed, achieved all business goals, etc.).
3. Identify the things you can change and the things you cannot.
4. What are you feeling?
5. How have you responded to your challenges and barriers?
6. How has this impacted you physically, emotionally, and mentally?

Realization

Being honest with yourself requires that you first commit to answering tough questions.

1. What is your ultimate business goal?

2. Have you achieved that goal?

3. Does the business have the potential to advance?

4. What skills or talents are necessary for business advancement?

5. Do you have the necessary skills needed to take it to its next level of advancement?

6. If you have the skills to take it to the next level how much time are you willing to commit to its advancement?

7. If you don't have the skills needed what are your options?

8. List your special skills and talents.

9. Can your special skills and talents be used beyond your business?

10. If yes, in what ways can your skills be used beyond your business?

REFLECTION

Think about the condition of your business and provide an explanation below.

Think about how you feel about the condition of your business and list what you are feeling below.

Think about the situation and the cause and or condition and provide an explanation below.

Analyze the situation to identify the cause of the situation (self, poor management, tragedy, lack of skills).

Think about the things you can change pertaining to the condition of your business and write below.

REALIZATION

What are the areas you have no control over?

CHAPTER 10

REFOCUS

When you understand the need for change, you are more likely to implement an exit strategy.

—LaToya Thurmond

Let's be sure we're all understanding the meaning of refocus:

> **re fo cus –** adjust the focus of (a lens or one's eyes); focus (attention or resources) on something new and different[4]

Captors conceal their identity by blindfolding their hostages. As the vision of the captive is impaired, it becomes more difficult to break free from captivity. As a result, the proximity of the exit cannot be discovered. Losing sight of business goals and vision can leave you in a hostage situation, unable to see beyond what you perceive. Ensnared in darkness and confusion, you spend significant energy focusing on undertakings without a clear vision. The lack of awareness is what will keep you stuck in a season of roaming without purpose.

---

[4] Refocus. Definition from Google, provided by Oxford Languages.

Once you realize how your emotions prevent you from moving forward, you then can make a conscious effort to refocus. According to Shepherd (2003), psychological and emotional effects have the potential to create barriers after a business failure. It is easy to become stuck in the cycle of negative thoughts and emotions. Thurmond (2019), finds that the learning process may be hindered by negative emotions and self-doubt. To make progress you have to refocus your attention and energy on addressing the challenges. Perhaps you have procrastinated and have failed to complete important tasks. Take inventory of all operational and administrative tasks that need to be finalized. As you move forward in accomplishing your responsibilities, you will experience a sense of freedom and will be one step closer to total release. Refocusing allowed me to see that completing daunting tasks were essential to my total deliverance.

This next section will provide you with tips and strategies to help you identify solutions. This process will look different for every business owner and will require focus and commitment. While you journey out of your business, you should connect with your strengths and talents. The same skills and talents you used to start your business will help you in transitioning out.

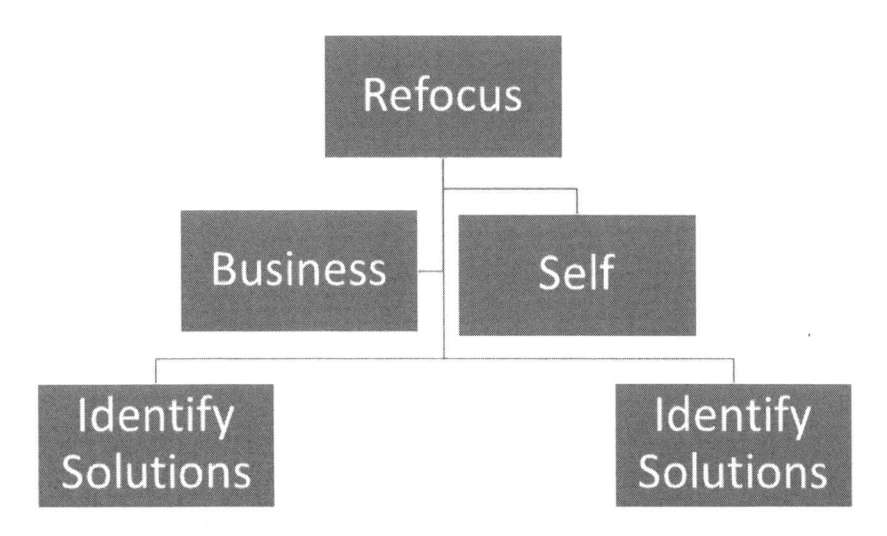

```
                    Refocus
                   /       \
            Business       Self
              |              |
         Identify         Identify
         Solutions        Solutions
```

I'm assuming that if you are working your way through this self-help book, you most likely do not have an exit strategy in place. Mentally, you may feel like you are going through a never-ending maze.

Business: Identify Solutions

I had gloated in having written a business plan that allowed me to acquire commercial property. When I look back over my experience, one of the biggest mistakes I made was not also creating an exit strategy. It is easy to pour all of your creativity and energy into what it will take to start the business. You can overlook what it will take to transition out of the business. Throughout creating short- and long-term goals, we often lack vision as to how we intend to exit.

Let's think of it from the perspective of life insurance. You purchase life insurance because you know that, inevitably, you will one day leave this earth. Part of your plans includes ensuring that your family is financially secure at the time of your death. If you can grasp that there needs to be a plan in place for the end of your life, why would you believe that your tenure in businesses will last forever? Unfortunately, whether it is business or death, we cannot determine how we exit, but we can make sure that we are prepared.

DeTienne (2010) states that one must have insight into the entrepreneurial exit to understand the entrepreneurial process. According to DeTienne and Cardon (2012), exiting out of the business is a vital part of the entrepreneurial journey. The course in which the founder of an organization removes themselves from the establishment created is identified as an entrepreneurial exit (DeTienne, 2010, p. 203). In other words, if you have been feeling as if letting go makes you a quitter, then I am here to let you know that exiting the business is part of the entrepreneurial process.

Listed below are possible reasons for entrepreneurial exits:

- Poor performance, unprofitable
- Met objectives and business goals
- Desire to exit
- Tragedy
- Change in the market

What's Blocking Your Exit?

Perhaps you feel as though you are failing to finish what you have started. According to research, entrepreneurial exit differs from failure (Hessels, Thurki & Van Der Zwan, 2018). In 2016, research showed that a common reasoning for entrepreneurial exit was the business being unprofitable and personal reasons (Global Entrepreneurship Monitor, 2017). Now is the time to refocus, acknowledge, and admit there are many reasons entrepreneurs exit.

Have you considered moving on from your business as a change where you are now assuming a new role? When you started your business, there were individuals waiting for you to show up to provide insight and creativity. There is now a different group of people waiting for you to show up to share your newfound knowledge and skills. You possess a new level of influence, and it may be time for you to pursue that new role. Leaving what you once knew for what is ahead can be tough, and the journey will look different for each individual who accepts the challenge.

Let's Get Moving!

There are a few ways you can exit your business while you may be left with only a few choices as to how you transition out of your business.

I encourage you to explore all the many ways you can successfully transition out of your business.

Merger and Acquisition

The process whereby your company is sold and combined to another company is called merger and acquisition. In merger, the two companies join to form a new corporation; one of the previous owners may still own a portion of the new corporation but is no longer in an active controlling role. As an example of acquisition, Company A purchases company B, and company B is now under the direction and leadership of company A.

Liquidation

In the case where you have no other choice but to take the nearest exit, you should just simply stop. This includes the liquidation of assets. For example, if I were managing a childcare center and ceased operations, I would liquidate all of my assets that could be sold, probably to another childcare center. It would be necessary that I find value in all my assets, such as vehicles, shelving, light fixtures, computers, office equipment, classroom equipment, building (if owned), etc.

Sale

In a sale, the owner would offer all the assets mentioned in the liquidation section and more. This would include the selling of intellectual property, process and procedures and policy. You would need to carefully think about the value that your company provides. When creating your sales pitch, consider why someone may want to purchase your business.

What opportunities would a new owner have by purchasing your establishment? While thinking about your business qualities, think about what it will take to maintain and further develop those qualities under new leadership. Would you consider working alongside the new owner to help them gain general understanding of the business? This would include learning how the business started, the successes, challenges, and current managerial procedures.

Family Succession Plan

The final plan for exiting that I want to provide is building a family legacy. Planning for your exit will require that you create a succession plan. You will first need to identify when you would like to exit out of the business. Will that be determined by the number of years of service or by a specific age at which you would like to retire from the business? This will also include identifying your successor and how they will be prepared to lead.

What Are You Waiting For?

When it comes to making decisions, we often struggle with wanting things to happen in perfect timing. Let me tell you there will not be a perfect time, just periods of rehashing, reconsidering, and many what-if thoughts. Making a dash for the exit will first require that you make a decision to let go and then create a solid plan. One last thing: *don't look back*!

Refocus: Negotiator

The negotiator shows up on the scene to communicate with the captor, who has posed a threat. This process takes great communication skills. The main objective of the negotiator is to arrive at a solution. The process of negotiation requires a great level of focus and strategic planning. The main role is to ensure there is no injury to people.

The negotiator determines the demands of the captor. If your business has you in a hostage situation, you will need to act as a negotiator. This will require that you first carefully assess the state of your business to determine what demands your immediate attention. This can be anything from outstanding tax liabilities, payroll, and mortgage or rent payments. You will need to prioritize the needs that have to be met while evaluating your ability to meet those demands. Unfortunately, sometimes you may not meet all demands, which will require that you identify the alternative outcomes.

For example, you may plan to terminate the lease three months earlier than you initially agreed. At the time of rereading the lease agreement, you notice that you will be held financially liable for those three months. However, you will not have the finances to pay the three months at the time of terminating the lease. Due to your inability to meet that demand, it will be required that you inform the property owner of your plans to terminate the lease and inability to make the three months payment per the agreement.

Do not sink into a place of procrastination. It will be important not only that you communicate your situation with the property owner but that you have a suggested solution. The outcome you seek will require that you have a plan in place, whether it be that you request an extension with a detailed timeline or that you ask that the payments be forgiven. In both cases whatever outcome you desire should benefit both you and the other party. In the above case, asking for forgiveness will require that you propose something that will benefit the property owner. Perhaps you know individuals looking for business space and can provide the property owner with a list of names. Assisting the property owner with finding a new tenant will serve as a benefit, especially where a new tenant meets all the tenant requirements and is ready to take over the lease immediately. Determining the need and desired outcome will allow you to create a plan that will allow you to effectively negotiate.

Once you have determined what you need and how you intend to make it a benefit for both parties, it is now time to open communication lines. This will require that you contact the stakeholder to arrange a time to meet. For some, fear of an undesired outcome will run rampant in your mind, and you may elect a more passive approach to reaching out. However, you must aggressively move forward in arranging time to discuss your decision to transition out of your business. You should understand that your choice to exit the business may create challenges for all who are directly connected to your business. Make the call, send the email—arrange time to have the discussion!

Review your plan

Once you know what you need and what you will do or provide to benefit the stakeholder, you are able to clearly and confidently articulate your goal to exit and how you intend to meet any outstanding debt. This will require preparation, and you should consider reviewing your plans and how you will open up this discussion. You will need to ensure that you clearly:

1. Communicate the effective date you are closing your business.
2. Communicate the reasoning for closing your business. If you are not comfortable sharing this information, be prepared to answer the question as to why you are closing in your discussion.
3. Acknowledge the demand (outstanding debt and agreements).
4. Communicate what you cannot do.

5. Communicate what you are willing to do (include the areas where they will find it beneficial).
6. Ask for what you need most.

Take time to practice and envision how you will present this information. You may find it helpful to practice how you will deliver the message with a coach, a friend who owns a business, or a close relative. Consider the potential questions that may arise and potential requests that may be asked of you. This will be a good time to think of your next steps if the conversation does not lead you to your desired outcome.

Things to consider:

1. Face-to-face discussion or a virtual meeting is better than emailing.
2. A signed agreement may be requested of you to ensure that you stay true to what you have proposed.
3. Don't commit to something you know you will not follow through on. You do not want to burn bridges—this may be a future stakeholder.

Self-Solutions

Corporations and larger institutions have the benefit of working to solve issues in a team setting. Small business owners work aggressively to resolve the problems at hand while battling negative emotions and ensuring that the operation is still moving. Bearing all the weight and pressure of a struggling business is exhausting. Stress interferes with your ability to focus on the development and execution of recovery plans. This experience taught me it is an absolute must to take care of yourself mentally, emotionally, and physically. Failing to do so will interfere with your ability to complete daily tasks.

I kept hearing the voice of one of my dissertation participants. "LaToya, it is important that people know that you must stay present." Your inability to focus due to fear, anxiety, and stress has a great ability to interfere with your ability to stay present. At this point, on your journey, you may have a long road ahead of you, but you must not neglect your greatest and most valuable asset. You!

When you are continually receiving bad news, and nothing seems to let up, it is easy to settle into a mode of stinking thinking. In time I found myself in a place where I was always looking for and expecting negativity. Eventually I found my faith at an all-time low.

Taking time to meditate with no interruptions should be part of your daily routine. Consider contacting a coach or even a therapist so you have the support you need to cope. Newton et al. (2008) recommended that a consulting psychologist play a significant role in assisting individuals in managing negative emotions. The constant accumulation of problems can turn into a direct assault on you mentally. You may not realize, but you may be experiencing grief as a result of an overflow of negative emotions.

Grief

Studies conducted by Singh, et al. (2007) and Cope (2011) revealed that grief follows worry, distress, fear, resentment, and often causes physiological symptoms including fatigue, high blood pressure, restlessness, and decreased weight. According to researchers, grief recovery is the time required before the reflection of events leading to loss no longer creates negative feelings and responses (Shepherd, Wiklund, and Haynie, 2009). Thurmond (2019) finds that once entrepreneurs arrive at a point of grieving, they must learn to cope with negative emotions before learning. In addition, Lazarus and Folkman (1984) identify coping as the process by which individuals manage negative emotions. Thereby, healthy relationships and support systems should be explored to determine its role in stability (Thurmond, 2019).

Do You Feel like Just Running Away?

I thought you might be thinking that. All the negative emotions, grief, and learning to cope are beyond overwhelming. However, you certainly cannot run away now. The company and your staff need you. However, maybe a day off and time away from the many tasks would do you some good. Perhaps a day at the gym or a nice walk will help you clear your mind.

Are you having moments when you feel like locking yourself up in the closet and throwing away the key? You may even feel as if people are watching your every move. Trust me; you are not under surveillance as you suspect. People most likely are unaware of your struggle because they are more concerned about their own. Besides, you are not alone in what you are experiencing. Some of the greatest have experienced business challenges and failures before reaching success:

- Oprah Winfrey
- Thomas Edison
- Milton Hershey (Hershey Company)
- Colonel Sanders (Kentucky Fried Chicken)
- Henry Ford

Alone time will give you some serenity. However, it is probably not best to lock yourself away unless you want to prolong the crisis. I found being away allowed me time to refocus so I could generate a game plan. Perhaps a getaway will give you the recharge that you need.

Refocus: Assess Your Needs

The time of personal reflection is a process that allows you to dig deep. It is a time for a reset, and most important, a much-needed time to prioritize what you need most. As you work your way through releasing your business, it is critical to assess your needs. Self-actualization is the need for growth and development that will propel you into your full potential. Maslow (1943) suggests that personal mistakes, weaknesses, and the improvement of growth and development can be identified by studying self-actualized people. According to Maslow, the need to meet physiological needs is the prerequisite to meeting overall self-actualization.

Your ability to identify unfulfilled needs will refocus your behavior towards meeting those needs to arrive at the level of self-actualization. Maslow's Hierarchy of Needs is illustrated by a pyramid that represents five essential human motivations. The lower needs are necessary to survive, and as those needs are met individuals are motivated to move to the next level in the hierarchy (Maslow, 1943).

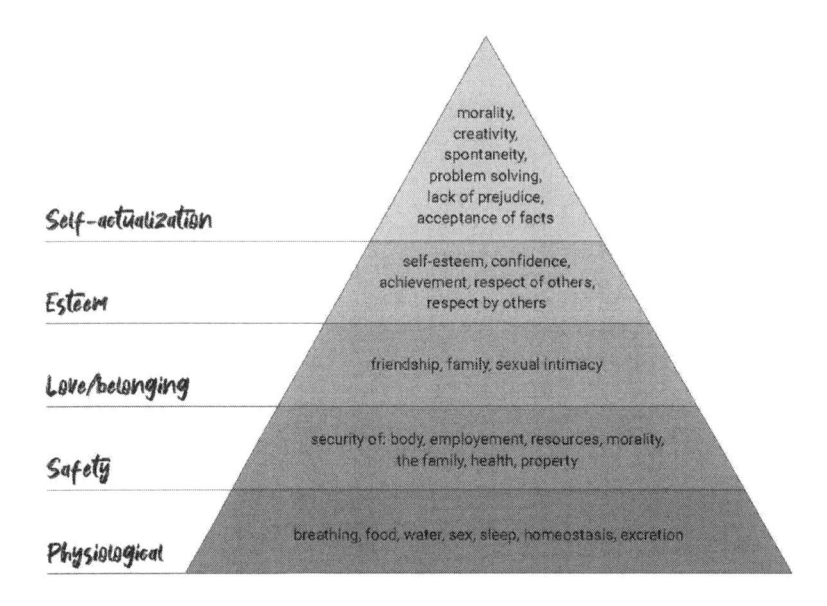

Self-actualization: morality, creativity, spontaneity, problem solving, lack of prejudice, acceptance of facts

Esteem: self-esteem, confidence, achievement, respect of others, respect by others

Love/belonging: friendship, family, sexual intimacy

Safety: security of: body, employement, resources, morality, the family, health, property

Physiological: breathing, food, water, sex, sleep, homeostasis, excretion

According to Thurmond (2019), recovery depends on the person and their level of motivation. Your ability to initiate motivational change will require that you first acquire knowledge and understanding of all five basic needs. Rouses (2004) suggest that as the most important needs are fulfilled the individual is motivated by the needs at the top.

As you learn more about the five basic needs, you will gain more insight into what you need most to reach a level of self-actualization. I am sure that your mind has been thrust into overdrive thinking of what you need. However, take the time to reflect upon each basic need to discover what is motivating your behavior as it applies to becoming a greater you.

Physiological Needs

"Entrepreneurs need a hiatus, allowing them to step away from the situation" (Cope, 2011). Just as any book has a break in the page at the end of the chapter, you too need to take a moment to pause. This would be a good time to make up for those times you denied yourself rest out of fear of what would potentially go wrong if you shut your eyes. When trying to survive, there is no room for pride. If you need food and water, you should reach out to community resources for assistance. Once your physiological needs have been met, you will then be motivated by meeting safety needs.

Safety Needs

Take time to evaluate your surroundings and living environment. Do you feel protected and secure? Are you feeling any sense of uncertainty? Perhaps the business was your only source of income, and now you face the growing concerns of being unemployed. If you agree to the above, then you need to access resources that will help you to feel safe. This may require that you reach out to the unemployment office, employment programs, or rental assistance if you do not have enough cash to keep you afloat.

You will need to determine your needs and reach out to the necessary resources and support services in your local community. Once you have found resources that stabilize your environment and provide you with safety, you will then find yourself motivated to meet esteem needs.

Ponder this! You may be in a space at the moment where you are feeling absolutely clueless about finding employment. Perhaps you even feel that your options are few depending on the economic climate. In interviewing entrepreneurs for "The Entrepreneurial Experience of Business Loss," I discovered that entrepreneurs are not afraid to start over. Don't be afraid to start over at a new place where you can regain your focus and confidence while using your skills.

Although you have been faced with many business challenges, you have developed a unique skill set that will be of great value to another organization while you work toward becoming more stable.

When you started dreaming about your business you thought of all the possibilities and options for success. You were most likely overjoyed and looked forward to your future in business. You may have even experienced major challenges that led you to the decision of starting a business. Wow! You have experience in fighting your way through challenges and have even more knowledge than you had before starting your business.

Start by simply reviewing your skill levels and how you could use those skills to provide for your need for safety. At this point, you have to spend some time envisioning a new you and all of those additional options you have. Trust me, whatever you may be challenged by may just be your way of escape. It's time to take every negative thought captive and start confessing openly that you have options. Once you realize you don't have to remain in the place you are in, then you will release your grip and let go. It is so hard to see now because you are remaining in a place of comfort. Once you release your grip, you will discover not only how much you have learned but also how much you have actually missed.

Have you neglected to take care of you? This would be a good time to evaluate your physical needs. Take time to schedule a checkup and any other important health exams you have ignored. An eye exam will be appropriate especially if you have spent a lot of time behind a computer completing administration functions. I don't mean to get personal, but when is the last time you visited your primary care physician? Now would be a great time to schedule a visit.

I challenge you to track what you are eating weekly. If you are anything like me, you will be amazed by how much fast food and junk you have got in the habit of eating. Throughout the day, take time to listen to your body and every ache and pain you have continued to disregard. I was shocked by how I was rumbling with headaches and working right through them because I was too busy to stop.

Love and Belonging

Perhaps you are in a place where your physical and safety needs are secure, but you just need love and belonging. Pouring all your energy into the business may have led to distant and fractured family relationships. Guilt may have you feeling that you are not deserving of being in a place of isolation while you heart craves for love and belonging.

Although some family ties may be broken and beyond repair, it is important that you pursue restoration with those that can be restored. It will take a positive mindset, perceiving what could be, and taking the steps to rebuild and strengthen relationships. Stinking thinking will have you focusing on the impossible and negative results. Perceiving family restoration will allow you to focus on positive reconnections with family and healed relationships.

Your commitment to reconnecting is what will move you forward into action. This may include you taking the initiative to reach out by making a phone call, sending a text message, or writing an email or letter. With all sincerity take time to admit your mistakes and the distance you have created. Perhaps even an apology for being emotionally unavailable is necessary. Share your story and how it has left you feeling so disconnected from those who matter most. It is my hope that you will find the love and sense of belonging that is so necessary during this time.

Now let's talk about friends!

For some, family may have been key to feeling the love and sense of belonging, while you may be seeking love and belonging in friendships.

It's hard to interact and be a great friend when being held hostage by your business. As a result, you may even have strained friendships that will never be the same. Although you may be feeling a sense of hopelessness and sadness from distant and damaged friendships, you can make new friendships that provide you with a sense of belonging. There is a world full of kind humans waiting and ready for you to show up. As a result, your journey to discovering new friendships will come with a new level of confidence and esteem.

Get connected. My journey consisted of reaching out to some of my friends who had experienced letting their businesses go. Being inspired by their stories of recovery is what put my shame to death. I was happy to be part of this amazing group of entrepreneurs who, in the process of recovery, had gained a wealth of knowledge from experience. I could see the new and improved me from afar. I had not only gained experience but also, I intended to share this experience with others somehow. This time of reconnecting allowed me to focus on what I had gained and not what I had lost. What I first was ashamed of, I found was very valuable as I would not be the last to experience this situation.

Finally, I beat shame by being transparent and letting my network know about my experience. While I was struggling to survive in my business, I had disconnected from community partners and contacts.

I had buried myself in my daily tasks and failed to keep in touch. I found it important to reconnect with this network as I knew many had the resources that would help relaunch my future.

Consider contacting a business coach to help you through your process. These valuable relationships will lead you to what is going on in the community and the surrounding areas. It is important that you know that the skills you used to start the business can thrust you to your next level. Building your confidence and networking skills will be critical in the rebirth and launching of a new and improved you.

Esteem

You may be standing in a palace of security, safety, and belonging, but your business experience has shattered your confidence. Letting go may have left you questioning your abilities and may have you feeling like a failure. Goodman (1978) finds that meeting and achieving the esteem needs occurs when self-confidence, strength, and a feeling of adequateness exist. Now that you have slowed down, you can focus on the many lessons learned. It is necessary that you take time to reflect on your experience.

Think about what went well while considering what went wrong. If you had to do it all over again, what would you change? How would you handle things differently? While you ponder over what you learned from managing the operation, don't forget to evaluate what you learned more about yourself in this process. I am sure there are skills and knowledge you have developed that you did not have before starting your business. Running a business is not for the faint at heart, and you stood tall and strong while doing the best you could to navigate business challenges.

You can use your experience to evolve into something greater. However, low self-confidence will keep you from applying what you have gained from your experience. This would be a good time to do some self-reflecting. You are your greatest asset.

I had been stuck in survival mode for five years with a mind on autopilot. It took a literal fire and flood for me to see that all of my potential, gifts, and talents were dying. Every thought, emotion, and feeling was temporary as I continued to encounter an array of challenges and occasional wins.

As the days of recovery continued, one morning, for the first time, I was enjoying the drive to the location. I rolled down the window to feel the breeze and capture a better view of the beautiful flowers starting to bloom. This was the first time in years I had been present in the moment. Although I did not know how things would end, I felt deep down within that all would be well. I can remember vividly paying close attention to the leaves on the trees and the sunny blue sky. Every day seemed like a roller coaster ride, but that day just seemed different.

While I was enjoying the beautiful day, the name of our loan credit analyst scrolled across my cell phone. To my surprise, my heart did not race, and my stomach did no summersaults. There was definitely something different happening.

The commercial property I had purchased had been partially funded by a nonprofit organization that provided business financing. I had been intentional about not missing a beat with this agency and ensured that I remained current with their payment. The credit analyst who managed our account was meticulous.

When trying to walk through a crisis, you do not have the time nor want the burden of additional stress and pressure. I was finally having a moment of peace, and I did not want this conversation to ruin my day. I debated whether I should answer the call. *It's time to stop walking in fear; the worst is behind you.*

"Hello."

"Hi, LaToya. How are you today?"

"I am well. How are you?"

"I am great," the credit analyst replied. "I am just calling today to get an update on how things are going."

It was always extremely stressful dealing with this analyst. Due to our IRS struggles, it was mandatory we provide monthly financial statements and verbal check-ins. With the small amount of money that was due and having never missed a payment, the entire process was just extreme.

I knew that she had a job to do, but I thought her tactics were borderline harassment.

It seemed like every holiday weekend always included a lengthy email with a laundry list of things to report. I mean, how unthoughtful. *You, Ms. Credit Analyst, are preparing for a nice, extended holiday weekend but not before making sure that I have a worrisome weekend. You have to be kidding me.*

Trust me. I preferred to deal with the IRS than this credit analyst. When she contacted me on LinkedIn, I was positive that I was dealing with a stalker. At the end of every phone conversation, I would think, *Where did they find her? I really need to get from under this debt.*" She was such a pit-bull credit analyst, I felt like I was indebted to her.

I answered, "Things are going great! We had a fire and a flood, and we are slowly recovering."

"Fire *and* flood! Oh, my goodness. What happened?" she asked.

"Some ice melted and seeped into the circuit breaker, igniting a fire."

"I hope everyone is okay."

"Yes, we are surviving," I said, thinking, *Anytime with the financial questions. 3. 2. 1—*

She was right on cue. "So how are you doing financially?"

"We have struggled in the last few months, but we are gradually turning things around."

"LaToya, I am sorry to hear this, she replied. "Why didn't you tell me?"

At that moment I felt myself going from my happy place to a ticking time bomb. My body tensed up, and I knew that the switch was getting ready to happen. "Did we ever miss a payment?"

"No."

"We are making all of our payments on time; therefore, I did not find it necessary to tell you."

The credit analyst replied, "LaToya, we could have offered you support."

"What support?" I blurted. "You people have no idea what it is like to walk through the fire of a business crisis. My job was to lead the organization through the problem. Informing you of the situation would only have put unnecessary pressure and stress on me with the hundred questions and demands. I did not know what was happening myself, so I knew I would not have answers for you, and I did not need to be hassled. I made sure I maintained the loan payments. Besides, this situation did not occur at the property you financed." I paused. "By the way, what support could you have offered?"

There was a silent pause, then she asked, "Well, where are your numbers now?"

"Once I get back to the office, I will provide that information to you." We were tracking numbers by the hour, but that day I was just through jumping at her every demand.

"Yes," she said. "The board will want to know this because they review your file monthly."

I answered, "You let the board know this one thing. The building is not their greatest asset; it is me. The building does not have the power, energy, emotional, and mental capacity to turn this crisis around. Please let them know that it is vital to ensure that their investment, meaning me, is emotionally and mentally sound. I have endured a lot over the last few months, and pushing me may just lead to me pulling out of all of this."

"LaToya, I know you have been through a lot, and we will support you however we can."

"Thank you. I will be in touch soon."

This phone call has gone down in history as one of the most defining moments in my life. I had found my confidence, and I was feeling free. I was at the point where I had nothing to lose, and I learned to release how I felt for my sanity. For years, I struggled with being able to confidently express how I felt about the entire process. When you fail to challenge the process, you are often pushed around. I wanted the credit analyst and the board to know that I was their greatest asset, and they should be concerned about my well-being. I was confident that I was the key to turning the situation around.

Mufasa, in *The Lion King*, gave some good advice: "Look inside yourself. You are more than what you have become. Remember who you are."

As I had grown attached to my business, I had lost touch with my strengths and abilities. My experience of wandering through the wilderness had become normal. Walking about as a drifter in my business presented many challenges. Although I didn't like the challenges, I had grown comfortable with them. Let me be honest: the challenges had developed into a routine struggle in my choice to become one with the struggle.

I forfeited my opportunity to grow, and I suppressed my strengths, creativity, and talents. The responsibilities of being a small business owner can be tough. You may have struggled to survive to the point where you have emptied out all of you. Taking time to refocus to remember who you are is so necessary at this part of your journey.

Power up! "If you don't know your worth, if you don't know your value, if you don't know how fantabulous you are—it's going to be hard for other people to see it. Being appreciative of self is beauty to me" (Kelly Rowland).

Self-Actualization

Do you have a hunger and desire for greatness? What will it take for you to evolve into your full potential? Have you considered your life purpose and all the things that will bring you joy? What you have experienced throughout your life's journey has prepared you for the top. As you have gained revelation of meeting the physiological, safety, and esteem needs, you are now ready for a self-actualization encounter.

Learning is Fundamental

Arriving at a point of realization is what will allow you to focus on the lessons learned. On your journey of exiting, you may have to come to a point of realizing so many things. Those areas will look different for each entrepreneur. After you have come to grips with your newfound knowledge as it applies to the well-being of you and your business, then you can refocus. The journey of refocus can feel like a self-discovery process where you move from an old mindset to embracing a new mindset. This period of refocus involves moments of pausing, reflecting, acknowledging, and evaluating valuable lessons learned.

    I learned so much about me and the errors I had made by reflecting. Where I was thinking I was moving forward, I was stuck in resolving routine challenges. Refocusing allowed me to ask myself the question, *Had I really been solving problems or was I only creating quick fixes?* I had later learned that the exhaustion from wandering without vision had weakened me; in a way I was only surviving. As a result, my limited mindset was holding me hostage, and I lost sight of my strengths and creativity. Learning will come by way of pausing, reflecting, assessing, and acknowledging which will eventually lead you to the desire to recreate.

Vision

Now it's time to chart your course!

This is your opportunity to explore and discover new territory. In other words, it is time to create new goals and seek out new challenges. Consider whether you want a fresh start in business or a new career path.

Let's Reimagine

Having a clear vision for your future is what will keep you from spinning in circles. This will require that you spend some time reimagining what your business and life could look like at this point of your journey. Journaling your thoughts would be a great way to capture your ideas. Depending on what works best for you, you can consider having two different journals that capture your thoughts for your business and your personal life. Listed below are some journal questions that you can consider.

Business

What have you learned from your experience as an entrepreneur?

In what ways can you apply those lessons?

- To an existing business?
- To a new business?
- To a new career path?

What opportunities have you discovered throughout your journey?

What does your business look like ten years from now?

REFOCUS

What does your business provide?

Who are your customers?

What is it that they need most?

How are their lives changed?

What are the strengths of your business?

What does your business need to avoid?

How is it managed differently from previously, or what is required to manage it if you are new?

What does your business need in order to grow?

Business Reimagination

Reimagine your business financially. What does it look like?

Reimagine how your business is managed. What does it look like?

Reimagine your staff and management team. What are they doing?

Reimagine your customers. What are they saying?

New Career Path (Option)

Where do you see yourself professionally five years from now?

What careers do you want to explore?

What are the skills that you are most confident using?

What are your strengths?

Why will an organization find your skills and strengths beneficial?

What is it that you need in order to grow professionally?

What career path would you like to pursue?

Career Path Imagination

Imagine you interviewing for a position, and describe your experience from the start of your day to the point of interviewing (provide great detail).

Imagine your workspace. What does it look like, feel like, and smell like?

Imagine yourself at your best while at work. What is it that you are doing?

Imagine yourself growing and advancing in your new career path. What does that look like? What does it sound like?

Personal

How has your experience impacted you personally?

What adjustments do you feel need to be made?

Where have you grown personally during this experience?

What sacrifices are you willing to make?

What sacrifices are you not willing to make?

Where do you imagine yourself ten years from now?

What is it that you need daily to support you on your journey?

How will you ensure that you get what you need?

Reimagine Your Life

Imagine what it's like to wake up in the morning. What are you thinking?

Imagine you trying something that you have never tried before. What does it look like?

Imagine you being around people that you love. What does it sound like?

Imagine you doing the one thing that you love the most. What emotions are you feeling?

***

Once you have spent some time journaling and visualizing, it is time to create a plan that will serve as your guide. For some, it will be creating or updating a business plan while others will create a plan to enter a new career path.

Once you have visualized the next chapter of your life, it is time to make moves. Identify opportunities and new roles that will allow you to use your entrepreneurial skill set. Whether you are starting a new business or entering into a new career path, this is a fresh start which will require a new mindset.

Take Action:

1. Identify and create a list of what matters most to you in this season of your life.
2. Determine what you need to focus on now so you may focus on what matters most.
3. Reconnect with yourself to determine what you need most and take care of your needs.
4. Pause and evaluate the business and life lessons learned.
5. Create the plan that works best for you based on what you desire and your needs.

Refocus

Refocusing includes: creating an exit plan OR reviewing a plan already developed and getting ready for your departure.

Creating an exit plan will allow for a smooth transition. This plan should include your goals for closure, which includes evaluating your departure goals.

Let's begin by just simply unloading all of your thoughts and ideas so you can have a clear focus. This will require that you plan to free yourself from all responsibilities for approximately an hour. You will want to carefully select a place free of distractions and clutter that will allow you to tap into the best version of you.

REFLECTION

Think about your needs and write down what you think *you* need most at this time below:

What do you need to focus on now so you may focus on what matters to you most?

CREATE YOUR PLAN

FREE YOUR MIND & THE REST WILL FOLLOW

Needs: Timer, blank poster size paper, colored markers, notebook. Additional Needs: Music, favorite beverage.

Date: _____ Place: _____

Time: _____ Approximate time: _____

Data Dump

Take twenty minutes to write down everything that comes to your mind you must address in exiting your business (Examples: staff, finances, debt, agreements, lenders, property owners, etc.).

In fifteen minutes try to label each item using the following:
1 = I got this
2 = This will be a challenge, and I need to think this through
3 = I need to seek out advice and explore my options

Using twenty-five minutes, review the items listed on your paper and then answer these questions for each concern:

1. What are your plans to address this issue and timeline?

2. What are you finding most challenging about what needs to be done? Do you have a coach or advisor to help you think it through?

    - Schedule a think-it-through session with coach or advisor.
    - Determine steps and task to complete and completion date.

3. Identify an expert who can assist you in evaluating your concern.

    - List questions and concerns
    - Reach out to the expert
    - Establish what's next, task, and completion dates.

FREE YOUR MIND AND THE REST WILL FOLLOW
SESSION 2

Needs: Timer, blank poster from Session 1

Take time to review the information gathered from the first session.

1. Determine an exit date goal
2. Review tasks that need to be completed and completion date
3. Evaluate Your exit options

RESOURCES

Closing a Business
- Close or Sell Your Business
  https://www.sba.gov/business-guide/manage-your-business/close-or-sell-your-business
- SBA.GOV
  https://www.sba.gov/category/stage-business/closing
- How to close a business (Quickbooks Guide) https://quickbooks.intuit.com/small-business/coronavirus/resources/a-10-step-checklist-for-closing-a-business/
- Closing A Business (IRS.GOV)
  https://www.irs.gov/businesses/small-businesses-self-employed/closing-a-business
- Closing Down Your Business
  https://www.findlaw.com/smallbusiness/closing-a-business/closing-down-your-business-a-chronology.html

Succession Planning
- Family Business Succession: 15 Guidelines - The Family Business Consulting Group (thefbcg.com)
- A Blueprint for Family Business Succession Planning https://businesslawtoday.org/2018/01/a-blueprint-for-family-business-succession-planning/

Merger Acquisition
- 1. Mergers and Acquisitions – M&A Definition (investopedia.com) https://www.investopedia.com/terms/m/mergersandacquisitions.asp
- 2. What Are Mergers and Acquisitions? Definitions and What You Need to Know-TheStreet
  https://www.thestreet.com/markets/mergers-and-acquisitions/what-are-mergers-and-acquisitions-14939523

REFOCUS

Selling a Business
- 1. 7 Steps to Selling Your Small Business (investopedia.com) https://www.investopedia.com/articles/pf/08/sell-small-business.asp
- 2. Close or sell your business (sba.gov) https://www.sba.gov/business-guide/manage-your-business/close-or-sell-your-business

Liquidating Assets
- Liquidate Definition https://www.investopedia.com/terms/l/liquidate.asp
- How to Liquidate a Closing Business's Assets https://www.nolo.com/legal-encyclopedia/free-books/small-business-book/ chapter12-7.html

CURRENT FINANCES

Bank	Account Type	Amount
Total Amount		

OUTSTANDING DEBT

Debt	Amount Due
Total Debt	

OUTSTANDING PAYROLL & TAXES

Employee	Total Hours Owed	Total Amount Owed
Total Payroll Debt		

ASSETS

Asset	Value	Sale Price
Total Liquidated Assets		
Total Finances + Total Liquidated Assets	=	

List three ways you can liquidate the assets listed:

1._____

2._____

3._____

Who should you notify and when do you plan to inform them of closing your business?

Notification List	Date	Method of Notification (emails, face to face, letter, phone)
Staff		
Clients		

TRACK YOUR PROGRESS

Get into action! It is time to move so you can complete the task before you move forward.

BUSINESS CLOSURE TASK TRACKER

Task	Who is Responsible	Who must be Contacted	Date Assigned	Date Due

OPERATION YOU!

Your most valuable asset has always been *you*!

Take Care of Your Needs
- 79 Self-Care Ideas (and Fun Activities and Routines You Deserve) https://liveboldandbloom.com/09/self-improvement/self-care-ideas
- 20 Simple and Real Ideas to Add to Your Self-Care Routine | SUCCESS https://www.success.com/20-simple-and-real-ideas-to-add-to-your-self-care-routine/
- How To Practice Self-Care: 10 Worksheets and 12 Ideas (positivepsychology.com) https://positivepsychology.com/self-care-worksheets/

Books
The Happier Approach: Be Kind to Yourself, Feel Happier, and Still Accomplish Your Goals, Nancy Jane Smith
Get Out of Your Head, Jennie Allen
Learned Optimism, Martin E. P. Seligman.
Losing You Is Not an Option Get Back Up and Fight, Nycole P. Lyles-Belton, PhD

Apps
- Calm
- Fabulous - Daily Self Care
- Headspace
- SWITCH App - Dr. Caroline Leaf

CHAPTER 11

RELAUNCH

The process of rebirth promotes the concept of entrepreneurial rebranding and the recreation of a new and improved entrepreneur.

—LaToya Thurmond

Like a phoenix rising out of the ashes fearless and free, you are ready to ascend. Prepare to embrace the new and improved life and reality that await you.

> **re launch** – reintroduce or restart (something, especially a product).[5]

Ultimately, relaunching is a process that requires both a new vision and preparation.

For some, that is never looking back but only moving forward. In my case, I moved from owning two businesses to one, which included stepping back and releasing responsibility. Besides, hovering over staff every moment of the day would have prevented their ability to grow.

---

[5] Relaunch. Definition from Google, provided by Oxford Languages.

One of the ultimate goals of any business owner is arriving at a point where you are no longer a necessity in the day-to-day operations. Choosing to let go allowed me to achieve that goal and fully embrace my role as entrepreneur and chief *visionaire*.

Take Action

Taking action will require that you not only have a plan but that you remain confident in your skills and abilities. My action plan required that I first reconnect with my network. I found it necessary to see what opportunities existed in my community and how I could contribute. What is your action plan? What does it require?

Once you develop your action plan, you must wake up each morning ready to take on the day. Some days you will feel stuck and uncertain of what your future holds, while on other days you will experience exciting breakthroughs. Each day is a new day, so commit yourself to starting fresh daily.

Get In Motion

Now that we were down to one location, it was easier for me to take action on rebranding the business and my personal brand. I had one center to oversee, which made it easier to reevaluate the vision and mission of the organization. I had been stuck in survival mode for years and had lost touch with what I was doing and why. Relaunching for me was introducing a new plan and direction for the center as well as for me personally.

During my business crisis I started LMT Consulting to survive financially. It became a challenge as I worked to manage a struggling business and personal finances. In reality I was juggling way too much and trying to focus on more than one thing at a time. Although my consulting contracts were keeping me afloat, I had no time to be intentional about developing the organization.

After carefully evaluating everything, I determined that it would be beneficial to be intentional about relaunching all three organizations that had been functioning but not at full potential. The relaunch consisted of me determining how the organizations could work together.

Relaunching included creating a new and improved mission and vision of where we were going and how we would get there. For years, I had led the organization with a survival mindset, so it took some time to recondition the staff to see beyond surviving the struggle. This also included executing a plan of action that would help us to get out of debt. In my effort to revive the organization, there was one thing that was helping, but it had a direct impact on me personally. Removing myself from the payroll had proved to work and had reduced monthly expenses; however, I could not survive financially. I had two choices: either eliminate the director and assume the position as director myself or use my skills and newfound knowledge to explore and create additional opportunities.

This was where I found it necessary to be intentional about relaunching my consulting company. That also included seeking out part-time employment opportunities. For years I had been stuck in the organization, trying to survive setbacks, challenges, and a failed economy, that I had put away my first love—training and development.

While in the struggle, I took notice of how I absolutely loved working with agencies and providing customized training. Those were the times when I felt I was actually applying the knowledge I gained from my Master's Degree in Adult Education. I was at a point of intentionally rebranding my business to include training and development for adults. The relaunch included starting fresh daily looking for opportunities, submitting conference proposals, completing train-the-trainer courses, facilitating trainings, leading roundtable discussions, presenting at seminars, and sharing my survival stories.

This was a whole new world that I was beginning, and it looked entirely different from early childhood education. In addition, I was working toward completing my dissertation, learning more about what made me happy, and finally gaining some wins. Within time, I started to discover a new me.

Change Can Be Scary!

It's one thing to come up with a new plan, but it's another to get out there and do it. As I held the plan of how we would get unstuck, I also needed to feel confident in the team that would be leading the charge. My experiences outside of the office had only been for a few hours perhaps one or two days out of the week. That was slowly changing to a few hours daily.

LaPre Enterprise had been on an overextended roller-coaster ride. Like a mother protecting her child from every twist, turn, and unexpected drop, I was uncomfortable with the thought of leaving the staff for contracted work or to work for another employer. Although I had a solid director in place, I was imagining all the things that could go wrong without me being there. *What if something happened and I had to leave in the middle of a presentation? What if they had to deal with a challenging parent? How can I stay abreast of everything that is happening without being there?* My mind raced and raced until I thought, *But what would happen if I do not take the risk to launch out?*

Then I would think about all the things that had already gone on while I was on-site. It was then that I realized I just needed a strong, solid team I could confidently lead at a distance. However, getting beyond my fear of trusting someone else with my business for even a short period of time was frightening. As I prepared to transition from being on-site on a regular basis, I created outlines of what should occur daily and who should handle what. That included holding brief check-ins while driving to my assignment, brief check-ins coming out of the door from the assignment, and quick how's-it-going text messages during short breaks and periods of waiting.

A New Beginning

One of my good friends worked at United Way and reached out to see if I would work part time as a campaign associate. The hours were flexible, and the position was only a five-month term. It involved connecting with area businesses in the community

Within a blink of an eye, I began working the part-time position and was learning new things. I decided this would be a good change for me, and the thought of being approached to work the position really boosted my confidence. I could work part time and gain additional experience, network, and not smother the management team I had put in place. Besides, I was financially drained, so this was also an opportunity for me to recover.

There was something called "taking a lunch," which was so unfamiliar to me. Working throughout the day nonstop interfered with my ability to see my own neglect. One day my good friend stopped by my cubicle and said, "Girl, I noticed that you hardly move. Please make sure that you are getting up and moving around. Take a walk or something. Are you even eating lunch?" That was an aha moment. It was another reminder of how I chose to deprive myself from basic needs such as food and water.

Back at the business, things were looking up. There were positive changes taking place, and the organization was beginning to excel. Finally meeting our financial goals, it was evident that consolidation had in fact worked. We were climbing out of debt, and shockingly, the business was bringing in more income than it had when it was operating with two centers. We were moving from a position of surviving to thriving. This was confirmation that I had made the right decision to consolidate. Finally, my fear of not meeting payroll was disappearing.

Change Is Good

My assignment at the nonprofit agency had one month left. It was bittersweet because I could feel myself needing a change. Three months prior, I had completed an online application for a part-time position as a business management learning success coach at the local college. To my surprise, I received an email from them informing me that I had been selected to interview for the position. This was groundbreaking news, and the opportunity presented itself just at that right time. As I said goodbye to newfound friends and colleagues, I accepted the coaching position and prepared myself for a new journey.

I was on the road to discovering the new and improved me, and the feeling of being away from the office finally set with ease.

This position involved coaching business students. Time spent with students and budding entrepreneurs encompassed sharing many of my success stories, including winning the Small Business Administration award for not only the southeast region of Wisconsin but the Midwest region of the country. I enjoyed highlighting my successes; however, I found sharing the struggles and failures more valuable.

The Good, the Bad, and the Ugly

Everyone wants to talk about success, but no one wants to talk about failure. Research has dedicated more time to evaluating entrepreneurial success while ignoring failure rates (Heinze, 2013; Singh et al., 2007). Statistical data shows that failure is common for business startups. I wanted to ensure that the student's realistic view demonstrated that growth could emerge out of failure as it does out of success. By creating a balance between success and failure, the students are aware of the risk, which empowers them to confront their greatest fear—failure.

I would always begin my *So You Are Thinking about Starting a Business* workshop by saying, "When you leave this session, you will feel one of two ways. There will be a feeling of excitement to pursue your business goals or you will run as fast as you can without looking back." I found it absolutely necessary to inform them of the good, the bad, and the ugly.

Ultimately, my personal goal was that once students graduated from their program, they possessed the confidence to start a new business. Encouraging individuals to face fear head-on provides them with bounce back power if a business failure occurs.

I was enjoying coaching and interacting with the students and facilitating workshops. However, I was going through a total transformation and was struggling with interacting with my colleagues at the college.

Initially upon entering the workplace, I had wrestled with working in teams. As an entrepreneur, I was used to directing a team and solving all major problems independently. My mentality was about protecting assets and intellectual property. I was accustomed to competitors stealing innovative ideas and passing them off as their own. I then was thrust into a world where absolutely everything was shared without question. As a visionary capable of providing great ideas, I was not open to sharing much. I had to constantly remind myself that I was now an employee hired to execute the vision of the employer.

Now I was in an environment where I worked with a collective group of individuals who excelled at execution. While trying to blend into this new environment, I was even more grateful for my support staff.

I thought I was doing pretty well as I had learned a little bit about packing a lunch from the nonprofit organization. Now I was being invited to local restaurants by my new colleagues who enjoyed working lunches. I sat quietly in meetings observing their interactions, how they solved problems, communicated, and interacted with supervisors. Perhaps I formed an opinion or two. Likewise, they had formed an opinion of me as being shy, standoffish, and reserved. Maybe their observation was based on me being distant in meetings and only contributing when I felt I had something valuable to say. In some ways, they were partially correct.

My shyness was actually calculating, my standoffishness was my survival instinct, and the possible assumption of my reservation was accurate. They were right but on the same note, I was summing them up based on their temperament, team mentality, and how they responded to conflict. Over time I would learn that I was partially correct, and I was grateful for my discernment. However, I was not only observing them, but I was also having my personal moments of self-reflection. I acknowledged there was so much more that I had yet to reveal and so much more that I could contribute beyond working with students.

However, I wanted no major responsibilities, pressure, or high expectations after making drastic changes to my business. This was a healing process for me, and I wanted to be free to empower students to achieve success both academically and in business. Now I realize I was totally limiting myself in this environment by not contributing. I shared knowledge and wisdom with my students but was holding back and denying my colleagues that same benefit.

When I began my journey working in this new environment, I felt like I had nothing to prove, and in reality, I did not have the energy. For years I had been stuck caring about the opinions of others, and I was not going back to the people-pleasing movement. The idea of climbing the ladder by gaining the approval and acceptance of others was exhausting. Eventually I learned that it was not about proving who I was as much as it was about sharing my knowledge, skills, and abilities. This experience was new, and it was stretching me in such a way that I often found this new environment uncomfortable. As time went on, I occasionally wondered if I could settle into working for the institution for the long haul.

As I continued to internalize my journey at this new and exciting place, I noticed how I was evolving. My perspective was changing as I continued to grow and develop. I learned that a limited mindset accustomed to struggle would no longer serve me as I continued the journey to rediscovering a greater me. I had to make a conscious effort to look for open doors when I had grown comfortable with them shutting. Where I had once accepted that my life, both professionally and personally, would be a constant struggle, I discovered that I had a choice; struggle did not have to be my lifestyle. While for me, it took going through an unhealthy state mentally, physically, and emotionally, that doesn't have to be the experience for every entrepreneur.

Relaunch: Broaden Your Horizon

Listen up! Liberation came by having a made-up mind that allowed me to make the best decision for myself at that point in my life. Of course, there was unfinished business that took me weeks, if not months, to rectify. However, gaining the courage to stand up to my inner critic to release the bonds that tied me was transformational. Through a continuous process of renewing my mind. I had experienced a transformation. This metamorphosis would no longer allow me to be controlled or defined by my business. In addition, I was destined to walk out of my self-imposed prison ready to explore the world.

Family

My life had been full of worries and responsibilities, and I could never find peace. Unfortunately, all of my business struggles always managed to find a comfortable spot in my home. I had to admit that I had missed out on the thing that mattered most, which was time spent with Shaun and the girls. The ones who would continue to exist if I had lost it all. As I fought to keep my business on life support, I needed to support the lives that were the beat to my heart. This was a challenge as I worked hard to be mentally present and provide my undivided attention. Relaunching family required that I take time to live in the moment as my two daughters had blossomed into young women within a blink of an eye.

A relaunch allowed me to see the phrase *what's for dinner, babe* as a gift of being a mother and a wife and having a partner willing to assume all roles in my absence. A relaunch included me stepping away from my long list of tasks and challenges for a much-needed break to the ice cream parlor with Shaun. Relaunching my family also included creating a safe haven in my home that could not be hindered by the outside world.

The new environment I created included fresh paint, live plants, and renovations from the inside out. I found joy in the shattering of the glass in the ten-foot dumpster as I rid my home of all the unnecessary junk. I connected the dots as I saw each item as a representation of all the things I had been holding on to. They had been merely taking up space and crowding my life. As I carried the items to the dumpster, things were becoming clear and as a family, we were seeing our way out of all the stress and cares of the world. While I got excited about creating this new environment, I appreciated the giggle chats my daughters had at night and once again my husband's never-ending concern of *What's for dinner, babe?*

Sisterhood

I found being the oldest sibling to come with a great level of responsibility and commitment. I found it my duty to stand strong for the both of us. Preneice is insightful and knowledgeable and has an appreciation for facts and logic. If you ever were to meet, her introduction would sound something like, Hello, my name is *Preneice, but you can call me Grace*. The pronunciation of her name could be a bit of a challenge, so she preferred the use of her middle name. In finding my exit and rediscovering a greater me, she helped me find that grace had been with me all along and was waiting for me on the other side.

A relaunch in sisterhood allowed me to see I could not only find strength but a friend in my sister. A relaunch in sisterhood allowed me to be vulnerable to allow my sister to take the leading role in showing me how to let go. As I showed my weakness, her strength showed up as a roaring lion, and it was then that I discovered that she too had just as much strength as I did and in some cases even more. A relaunch was having the courage to be weak, so someone else could take their rightful place in being strong.

A relaunch in sisterhood was not only giving advice and encouragement but also receiving it. A relaunch in sisterhood was learning from your sister that the most important thing in life is having a family to love and cherish. Finally, a relaunch in sisterhood for me was realizing that my sister was my biggest and most trusted supporter, who believed in me more than I did and who wanted to see me happy, not bound. This relaunch allowed me to find the value in sisterhood and the joy of having a forever friend and confidant of a lifetime.

Friendships

A relaunch in friendships was something that I have come to value and appreciate. Making new friends while hanging on to a few of the old was enriching. Along the journey I discovered new friends that in some peculiar way welcomed me into the world of being free from captivity. While my old friends applauded me and stood in awe of my battle scars, my new friends taught me how to live through them. In reality, I had been in a place where I was accustomed to pouring all of my energy to the point of depletion.

In my mind, I found it inexcusable to be shaken by anything. I had so much responsibility to bear, and it didn't allow me to stop and feel the pain. A relaunch in friendships gave me permission to feel that pain as my newfound friends stuck close like newfound sisters and sometimes even like a mother. Late-night conversations and a constant exchange of encouragement was what I needed in my new world of freedom.

Travel

A relaunch was making a conscious decision and effort to enjoy life. From the point of working in the family business until I had decided to consolidate, it had been twenty years. Within those twenty years, a vacation included leaving on a Thursday night and returning on a Monday morning. The last time I could remember taking a real vacation was in my childhood. Guilt was always at the helm in my mind when I considered taking a vacation.

A relaunch was seeing life as one that needed to be explored. Most important, it was having the desire to try new things and see how others lived. My travel initiation included sailing on the Bahamas' deep blue sea while flying in the friendly skies to eight states in one year. Finally, I was remaining present during them all. Traveling was something I was learning to not only do but rather enjoy.

Confidence

Although my confidence was fractured, I never stopped planting seeds of hope. My relaunch was regaining consciousness as a visionary able to speak life into the lives of others while giving birth to innovative concepts. Finally, my confidence relaunch was committing to never lose faith in the small voice that provides me with divine knowledge, creativity, and insight. A relaunch required that I step back to acknowledge that I was a survivor and that the favor and hand of God rests upon my life.

What Do You Need to Relaunch?

My experience taught me that relaunching was not only restarting a business or career but having a new perspective on life. A few areas I have shared included family, friendships, and confidence. Now would be a good time for you to consider the areas in your life that need a fresh start.

Relaunch requires that you:

1. Seek help as you begin your new journey.
2. Try something beyond what you have always known.
3. Use what you have learned from your experience to push you further into your destiny.
4. Recognize that you may need to make adjustments as to how you think.
5. Be intentional and stay committed to the things you need and what matters to you most.

Relaunch

Your transformation will require that you create a plan to identify your steps.

List (3) areas in your life that need a relaunch.

1._____

2._____

3._____

TAKE ACTION

RELAUNCH #1

Specific Goal (Measurable, Attainable, Realistic, Time-bound):

Action Steps:

1._____

2._____

3._____

RELAUNCH #2

Specific Goal (Measurable, Attainable, Realistic, Time-bound):

Action Steps:

1._____

2._____

3._____

RELAUNCH #3

Specific Goal (Measurable, Attainable, Realistic, Time-bound):

Action Steps:

1._____

2._____

3._____

List (5) areas of focus for your new journey and (5) accountability partners/coaches to help guide you along your new journey and assist you in these areas on your journey.

Example (Career, family, spirituality, etc.)   Jane Doe

1._____

2._____

3._____

4._____

5._____

DON'T STOP DREAMING

What are (3) things you have never done or always wanted to do?

1._____

2._____

3._____

How can you use the lessons you have learned from your experience on your new journey?

Stay connected to the things that matter to you most!

1. *Braving the Wilderness,* Brené Brown

2. *Dare to Lead,* Brené Brown

3. *Don't Settle for Safe – Embracing the Uncomfortable to Become Unstoppable,* SarahJakes Roberts

REFERENCE

DeTienne D. R. (2010) Entrepreneurial exit as a critical component of the entrepreneurial process: theoretical development. *J Bus Venturing,* 25(2):203–215

CHAPTER 12

CONCLUSION

The process of introspective analysis calls forth many lessons through the experience of business failure and ways in which these could be applied to a new journey.

—LaToya Thurmond

Four years after closing the location, I had completed my PhD, survived a business loss, and was now working full time in higher education. I found myself more engaged at home with my family and was discovering a new and improved me.

The business was continuously progressing, and I was modifying our business plan and refocusing. One of those changes included focusing more on A&S Unlimited Solutions, the nonprofit agency that started in 2009 but quickly was put on pause after experiencing the economic crisis. A&S Unlimited Solutions offers parent provider support and case management programming to LaPre Enterprises.

Over the years we created a mentorship program for teens and teenage moms. They soaked up wisdom and knowledge as if they were dry sponges. Many of them gained the necessary credentialing and education to work in the business. As the organization evolved, one of the teens blossomed into a strong, detail-oriented, no-nonsense

CONCLUSION

leader. The change became more apparent when she said with a sense of superiority, "Ms. LaToya, what happened to you? You used to be a brick wall; now you have turned into a marshmallow."

I look at tolerance and patience as my new acquired skills. She only knew me as a no-nonsense enforcer. I took a few moments to think about her question. I was perplexed and surprised by her frankness. I laughed it off and told her people change. I went home that night, thinking about her question. It hit me, and I felt free acknowledging and accepting something that I would have once denied. It was simple. After years of trying to survive in business, I fizzled out and lost my passion.

Many employees and administrative staff had come and gone. Like a revolving door, some returned and eventually left again. I was determined to hold on to the family legacy that had existed for twenty-five years. Leading an organization through turbulent times without a solid support system had weighed heavily on me. On the other hand, I had gained so much knowledge and experience in the struggle.

Coming to the point of realization while learning to refocus my time and attention on new opportunities is just what I needed to give birth to new aspirations. More than ever, I found my passion restored, refueled, and redefined. Realization requires that you understand the need for change. Refocus encourages a concentrated effort to pick up the pieces so that you can move beyond emotional distress while rebirth promotes the re-creation of a new and improved you. Relaunching allows you to start over again with confidence while walking freely on your new journey.

Deciding to let go was one of the most challenging choices of my life. I had finally made up my mind that letting go was the one thing standing in the way of me following the blueprint that God had designed for my life. Unable to see the road ahead, I walked by faith and not by sight. Today you can make that same decision. You can cling to the things holding you hostage or choose to let go and be free.

The choice is yours.

DEFINITION OF TERMS

The following definitions are taken from *Oxford Languages* and were accessed through a Google search, with the exception of asterisked terms (*), which are paraphrased in the author's own words or widely accepted definitions across the financial community.

anxiety – a feeling of worry, nervousness, or unease, typically about an imminent event or something with an uncertain outcome.
asset – property owned by a person or company, regarded as having value and available to meet debts, commitments, or legacies.
consolidation – the action or process of combining a number of things into a single more effective or coherent whole.
corporation – a company or group of people authorized to act as a single entity (legally a person) and recognized as such in law.
entrepreneurship – the activity of setting up a business or businesses, taking on financial risks in the hope of profit.
exit plan* – a means of leaving one's current situation, either after a predetermined objective has been achieved, or as a strategy to mitigate failure.
financial analyst* – a person whose job is to assess the financial condition of a business or asset to determine if it is a sound investment.
financial statements* – (or financial reports) formal records of the financial activities and position of a business, person, or other entity.
freedom – the power or right to act, speak, or think as one wants without hindrance or restraint.
guilt – a feeling of having done wrong or failed in an obligation.

hostage – a person seized or held as security for the fulfillment of a condition.

liquidate – wind up the affairs of (a company or firm) by ascertaining liabilities and apportioning assets.

metamorphosis – a change of the form or nature of a thing or person into a completely different one, by natural or supernatural means.

realization – an act of becoming fully aware of something as a fact.

refocus – focus (attention or resources) on something new or different.

relaunch – reintroduce or restart (something, especially a product).

self-imprisoned* – in a prison of our own making that limits us in some way, whether we're conscious of it or not.

stagnant – showing no activity; dull and sluggish.

stakeholder – a person with an interest or concern in something, especially a business.

succession planning* – a process for identifying and developing new leaders who can replace old leaders when they leave, retire, or die.

REFERENCES

Baron, R. A. (2008).The role of affect in the entrepreneurial process. *Academy of Management Review*, *33*(2), 328–340.

Buttner, E. (1992). Entrepreneurial stress: Is it hazardous to your health? *Journal of Managerial Issues*, *4*(2), 223–240.

Cardon, M. S., & Patel, P. C. (2015). Is stress worth it? Stress-related health and wealth trade-offs for entrepreneurs. *Applied Psychology: An International Review*, *64*(2), 379–420. https://doi.org/10.1111/apps.12021.

Cope, J. (2011). Entrepreneurial learning from failure: An interpretative phenomenological analysis. *Journal of Business Venturing, 26* (6), 604–62. https://doi-org.library.capella.edu/10.1016/j.jbusvent.2010.06.002

DeTienne, D. R. (2010). Entrepreneurial exit as a critical component of the entrepreneurial process: Theoretical development. *Journal of Business Venturing*, *25*(2), 203–215.

DeTienne, D. R., & Cardon, M. S. (2012). Impact founder experience on exit intentions. *Small Business Economics*, *38*(4), 351–374.

Folkman, S., & Lazarus, R. (1985). If it changes it must be a process: Study of emotion and coping during three stages of a college examination. *Journal of Personality and Social Psychology*, *48*, 150–170

Global Entrepreneurship Monitor. (2017). Global report 2016/2017. Retrieved from http://gemconsortium.org/report/49812.

Goldsby, M. G., Kuratko, D. F., & Bishop, J. W. (2005). Entrepreneurship and fitness: An examination of rigorous exercise and goal attainment among small business owners. *Journal of Small Business Management, 43*(1), 78–93.

Heinze, I. (2013). Entrepreneur sense-making of business failure. *Small Enterprise Research*, 20(1), 21-39. doi: 10.5172/ser.2013.20.1.21

Hessels, J., Rietveld, C. A., Thurik, A. R., & Van der Zwan, P. (2018). Depression and entrepreneurial exit. *Academy of Management Perspectives, 32*(3), 323–339. https://doi.org/10.5465/amp.2016.0183.

Lee, Y. G., Jasper, C. R., & Goebel, K. P. (2003). A profile of succession planning among family business owners. *Journal of Financial Counseling and Planning, 14*(2), 31–41. Retrieved from https://search.proquest.com/docview/1355867058?accountid=36783.

Lazarus, R. S., & Folkman, S. (1984). Stress, appraisal, and coping. New York, NY: Springer.

Lewin, K. (1958). Group decision and social change. in E. E. Maccoby, T. M. Newcomb, & E. L. Hartley (Eds.), *Readings in Social Psychology* (pp. 197-211). New York, NY: Holt, Rinehart and Winston.

McGrath, R.G (1999) Falling forward: real options reasoning and entrepreneurial failure. *Academy of Management Review* 24(1): 13. doi: 10.5465/AMR.1999.1580438

Miller, D. (2015). A downside to the entrepreneurial personality? *Entrepreneurship Theory and Practice, 39*(1), 1–8.

Murdock, Mike. *The Business Woman's Topical Bible*, 2002. The Wisdom Center. page.377 #100

Shepherd, D. A., Wiklund, J., & Haynie, J. M. (2009). Moving forward: Balancing the financial and emotional costs of business failure. *Journal of Business Venturing* 24(2), 134-148. https://doiorg.library.capella.edu/10.1016/j.jbusvent.2007.10.002

REFERENCES

Singh, S., Corner, P., & Pavlovich, K. (2007). Coping with entrepreneurial failure. *Journal of Management and Organization*, 13(4), 331-34. Retrieved from http://library.capella.edu/login?qurl=https%3A%2F%2Fsearch.proquest.com%2Fdocviw%2F233253125%3Fa

Spivack, A. J., & McKelvie, A. (2018). Entrepreneurship addiction: Shedding light on the manifestation of the "dark side" in work-behavior patterns. *Academy of Management Perspectives*, 32(3), 358–378. https://doi.org/10.5465/amp.2016.0185.

Stephan, U. (2018). Entrepreneurs' mental health and well-being: A review and research agenda. Academy of Management Perspectives, 32(3), 290–322. https://doi.org/10.5465/amp.2017.0001.

Thurmond, L. R. (2019). The entrepreneurial experience of business loss: Grounded theory (Order No. 13806894). Available from ProQuest Dissertations & Theses Global. (2195588239). Retrieved from https://www.proquest.com/dissertations-theses/entrepreneurial-experience-business-loss-grounded/docview/2195588239/se-2?accountid=36783